D0578002

Breed Lover's Guide™

MASTIFF

A Practical Guide for the Mastiff Lover

Elaine Waldorf Gewirtz

Mastiff

Project Team
Editor: Heather Russell-Revesz
Copy Editor: Joann Woy
Indexer: Sonja Armstrong
Designer: Mike Bencze
Series Designer: Mary Ann Kahn

TFH Publications®
President/CEO: Glen S. Axelrod
Executive Vice President: Mark E. Johnson
Publisher: Albert Connelly, Jr.
Associate Publisher: Stephanie Fornino

TFH Publications, Inc.®
One TFH Plaza
Third and Union Avenues
Neptune City, NJ 07753

Copyright © 2014 by TFH Publications, Inc.

Printed and bound in China
14 15 16 17 18 1 3 5 7 9 8 6 4 2

Library of Congress Cataloging-in-Publication Data
Gewirtz, Elaine Waldorf.
  Mastiff / Elaine Waldorf Gewirtz.
      p. cm.
  Includes index.
  ISBN 978-0-7938-4185-1 (alk. paper)
  1. Mastiff. I. Title.
  SF429.M36G49 2014
  636.73--dc23
                          2011042487

The Leader In Responsible Animal Care For Over 50 Years!®
www.tfh.com

Table of Contents

Chapter
1

History of
the Mastiff

One look at the imposing Mastiff with that wide grin and little bit of drool that appears when he's waiting for a treat and it's hard to imagine his ancestors' lives 5,000 years ago. Those dogs protected their masters, fought as gladiators, helped hunters, and guarded flocks. They moved cattle, lived outdoors, and pulled carts filled with war weapons. These Mastiff-types bear only a slight resemblance to the Mastiff breed we share our homes with today.

Like many old breeds, the precise origin of the Mastiff is not documented for verification. Rather, legends are perpetuated and perhaps even embellished over time through a mixture of oral history, folklore, and archeology. However, one fact is universally acknowledged—the Mastiff is a very ancient breed.

Like many old breeds, the precise origin of the Mastiff is not documented for verification.

TIMELINE

- **2500 B.C.E.:** Early illustrations of Mastiff-type dogs hunting lions in the desert near the Tigris River appear in Babylonian bas-reliefs in the mountains of Asia.

- **1211 B.C.E:** First written mention of Mastiffs in a document written in China.

- **218 B.C.E.:** When Hannibal crossed the Alps, he took several battalions of trained war Mastiffs, who crossed with local dogs and produced other breeds such as the St. Bernard.

- **350 B.C.E.:** Aristotle mentions the Molosser in a list of "most useful" breeds.

- **1215–1294:** Marco Polo wrote about Kublai Khan owning 5,000 Mastiffs used for hunting and war.

- **1377–1399:** The Legh family of Lyme Hall, Cheshire, kept and bred Mastiffs.

- **1415:** A Mastiff guarded her master, Sir Piers Legh of Lyme Hall at the Battle of Agincourt, until he was rescued.

- **1584–1590:** Mastiffs accompanied Englishmen to America and are mentioned in the chronicle of Sir Walter Raleigh's expedition.

- **1603:** King James I sent two Lyme Hall Mastiffs to Phillip II of Spain as a gift.

- **1835:** Dogfighting, bull- and bear-baiting were outlawed.

- **1860:** Six Mastiffs first exhibited at dog shows at Birmingham.

- **1879:** The first American Mastiff Club was formed, but later disbanded.

- **1883:** The Old English Mastiff Club was formed in England and established the breed standard; Mastiffs began exportation to America.

- **1885:** The Mastiff is recognized by the American Kennel Club. The first registered Mastiff was a dog named Bayard.

- **1920:** The Mastiff becomes nearly extinct in England because of World War I; entire kennels were euthanized because of extreme food shortages.

- **1929:** The Mastiff Club of America (MCOA) was established.

- **1945:** Few Mastiffs in England exist. Canadian and U.S. dogs were exported to England to increase the breed. Sally of Coldblow was the first Mastiff bred after World War II. Her offspring revived the breed in Britain.

Origins of the Mastiff

The Babylonians first used mud to depict a Mastiff-type dog in hunting and war scenes. Later, Assyrians repeated the scenes with two varieties of Mastiffs. Stone-carved sculptures in the mountainous caves of Asia and inside the tombs of Assyrian kings bore witness to Mastiff-like dogs who inhabited the terrain as far back as 2500 B.C.E.

These early Mastiff types were recognized as a molosser or molossus, and characterized by thick skulls, oversized feet, and foreboding expressions. Many different names were used for Mastiff-type dogs and the word Mastiff was used to describe the work they did. As hunters, fighters, and protectors, their qualities of strength, endurance, intelligence, and courage survived over time and still exist in today's Mastiffs.

Traveling Dogs

Traders to Asia carried the Mastiff-type dogs to the other parts of the world, including the Mediterranean, the Middle East, and Russia. A 1211 B.C.E. document mentions a Mastiff in China, and the Tibetan and Mongolian Mastiffs originated from these early dogs. The description of three-headed Cerberus, guardian of Hades in Greek mythology, had ferocious Mastiff-like attributes.

When Hannibal Barca, a Carthaginian military commander and leader of the Roman armies, attempted to establish supremacy over Rome and other great kingdoms in 218 B.C.E., he took along 30,000 to 40,000 troops, 40 war-trained elephants, and Mastiff-like dogs. The arduous 15-day journey crossed over the Pyrenees and the Alps into northern Italy, encountering snowstorms, landslides, and hostile mountain tribes. That many of these dogs survived the journey is a testament to their strength and loyalty. Possessing a strong guarding instinct, they protected the camp from invaders and were proficient at herding cattle used to supply the troops and at pulling munitions carts.

Later, Mastiffs mixed with other breeds and produced Mastiff crosses. These included the Alpine Mastiff, which later became the St. Bernard; the Bullmastiff; the Great Pyrenees; the Newfoundland; and the Rottweiler. The Doberman Pinscher, Great Dane, Bulldog, and Boxer also claim Mastiff ancestry, as do the American Pit Bull Terrier, Staffordshire Bull Terrier, Boston Terrier, French Bulldog, Pug, and the Chow Chow. Other breeds related to the Mastiff are the Dogo Argentino, Dogue de Bordeaux, Fila Brasileiro, Tibetan Mastiff, Neapolitan Mastiff, Spanish Mastiff, Pyrenean Mastiff, Bernese Mountain Dog, Greater Swiss Mountain Dog, Cane Corso, Entelbucher, Newfoundland, Tosa Inu, and Leonberger.

The forebears of today's Mastiff lived in Britain. They were strong canines who worked and fought alongside their British caretakers during battle. Noted in Caesar's account when he invaded Britain in 55 B.C.E., the powerful dogs possessed guarding instinct and were willing workers. The British Mastiffs so impressed the invading Romans that they brought these dogs back to Rome to fight in the Colosseum against human gladiators and wild animals, for the entertainment of nobility.

The Mastiff in England

In 1014, the Mastiff was one of a few breeds mentioned in England's Forest Laws, the country's first written statutes.

A Mastiff was recorded as coming over on the Mayflower in 1620.

WHAT IS A BREED CLUB?

The Mastiff Club of America (MCOA) is the national organization of Mastiff breeders and owners throughout the United States. Under the auspices of the American Kennel Club (AKC), the MCOA serves as a parent club for regional Mastiff clubs and helps to preserve the health and welfare of the breed. Under AKC guidelines, this association of fanciers wrote the original breed standard and is responsible for maintaining and revising it when necessary.

The MCOA and the regional clubs encourage and promote the quality breeding of purebred Mastiffs, provide information to the public about the breed, and sponsor conformation and performance dog shows promoting good sportsmanship. Mastiff owners share their camaraderie about the breed and as a result, learn more about Mastiffs and derive support from one another.

To join the MCOA, Mastiff owners must apply for membership and agree to abide by the MCOA Code of Ethics, the Constitution and Bylaws, and the AKC rules.

Established by King Canute, the laws contain more than 8,000 words about Mastiffs. The dogs were prohibited from hunting in the large wooded areas reserved for the nobility. To prevent the starving population from using Mastiffs for hunting, the laws empowered the tax collector to check that the middle toes of each Mastiff's front foot were removed. This prevented the dog from running fast enough to catch deer, which belonged to royalty.

During the Elizabethan era (1558–1603), the Mastiff was used to fight bears, bulls, lions, and tigers to entertain the Queen. In 1835, the Parliament voted to outlaw this cruel sport. At the same time, the Dukes of Devonshire and Sutherland selectively bred Mastiffs and helped develop the breed. The Legh family of Lyme Hall, Cheshire, helped establish the Mastiff as it appears today.

Dog shows became popular in the mid-1800s, with 63 Mastiffs entered in a show in Birmingham in 1871. Wealthy people kept and bred Mastiffs, and started the first recorded pedigrees. In 1883, fanciers formed the Old English Mastiff Club. These dogs were registered with The Kennel Club in England. In the mid to late 1800s, European dog fanciers attempted to standardize dog breeds according to the traits for which they were bred, and the Mastiff breed standard began to take shape.

World Wars I and II took their toll on the Mastiff, as well as on other breeds and their owners. Food shortages made it too costly to keep a Mastiff, and only butchers could afford to feed them their meat scraps. As a result, the breed became nearly extinct until after World War II, when the United States and Canada sent Mastiff stock to Britain to revive the breed.

Breed History in the United States

When 25-year-old John Goodman crossed the Atlantic on the Mayflower from Southampton, England, to Plymouth, Massachusetts, in 1620, the pilgrim brought along two dogs—a Mastiff and an English Springer Spaniel. Although there may have been other dogs aboard the ship, they were not recorded. Without listing their names, these two breeds were the only ones documented in Goodman's journal titled "Mourt's Relation." During the immigrants' first harsh winter in Cape Cod, the dogs helped find and retrieve game. Because of their service, they are acknowledged in the records of the founding of Plymouth Colony.

From colonial times, interest in the breed increased into the late 1800s. The first American Mastiff Club was formed in 1879, and the breed was recognized by the American Kennel Club (AKC) in 1885. Bayard was the first Mastiff registered. The club later disbanded but in 1929, the Mastiff Club of America (MCOA) was organized.

Popularity

During the 1960s, 1970s, and 1980s, the breed's popularity increased, but dipped in later years. According to AKC registration statistics in 2000, Mastiffs ranked 39th in popularity. Five years later, they were 33rd. In 2009, they climbed six places to 27th and edged down slightly only one place in 2010.

Working Dog Extraordinaire

The AKC divides all breeds into groups according to the jobs they were bred to perform. Each group has a history, and the members of the group share some common traits.

The Mastiff belongs to the Working Group. This group consists of dogs bred for protection, size, and strength. Working group puppies require training and socialization so they can live amiably with their families. Adult working group dogs need daily moderate exercise, continual training throughout adulthood, and careful management around children and other pets.

It helps when owners are confident and experienced with large, powerful dogs, and have the time and dedication for training. When understood and managed correctly, working dogs are nonaggressive and loyal partners to the people they respect.

What Is an American Mastiff?

The purebred Mastiff registered by the AKC is also known as the English Mastiff. It represents centuries of breeding to produce predictable behavior and physical characteristics.

An American Mastiff is a mixed "designer" breed, the result of a cross-breeding between an English Mastiff and an Anatolian Shepherd or another breed, such as an American Pit Bull Terrier or a Neapolitan Mastiff.

If a breeder tells you she has produced this new-breed Mastiff after only a few generations and that it has smaller jowls

Historically, Mastiffs are an integral part of royal families, and they are represented in art, literature, and collectibles.

Ask the Expert

Q: What is the best way to adopt a Mastiff?

A: If you're interested in adopting an older Mastiff, contact the Mastiff Club of America (MCOA). We help place stray or abandoned Mastiffs by working with several MCOA regional Mastiff rescue groups located throughout the United States. We also work with Mastiff owners who for any reason can no longer provide a home for their dog. It seems there are always Mastiffs who need good homes.

In 2005, the MCOA formed a tax exempt (501C-3) corporation in Virginia to coordinate rescue and placement of English Mastiffs.

In the past, people have given up Mastiffs due to a divorce or a death in the family, when no one is able to care for the dog. Or, sometimes people purchase a Mastiff puppy and realize a year later that it has gone from an 18-pound (8-kg) puppy to a 100-pound (45-kg) plus-size dog that they really don't have room for.

Today, most of the dogs needing new homes are victims of financial issues. Lately, because of the poor economy, people are calling us to help place their Mastiffs when they lose their homes and can't find a rental property that will permit a dog the size of a Mastiff.

Fortunately, once we find a new household, very few Mastiffs get bounced from place to place. We have a very thorough screening process.

To adopt a Mastiff, it's best to read our website and fill out and submit the Family Profile Adoption Application (www.mastiff.org). We're not prying into your personal life, but we want to make sure that you are prepared for the responsibilities of caring for a Mastiff. One of our rescue coordinators will contact you and make arrangements to visit your home.

You can also check the regional club rescue websites, which are linked into the MCOA website, for information about Mastiffs needing homes. Many of these dogs are placed with foster families who observe their personalities and can provide information about them.

—Charles Cuthbert, Mastiff Club of America (MCOA) rescue coordinator and doesn't drool, question this claim. There is no guarantee that every puppy of this mixed breeding will possess these traits. Developing any new breed takes several decades of dedication to firmly fix the characteristics that identify it. It's a myth, too, that an American Mastiff—or any mixed breed for that matter—is any healthier than the original breed.

Canine Stars

In television and movies, Mastiffs make Hollywood magic. Their amiable nature and presence gives them an edge as canine actors. In the 1993 movie, *The Sandlot*, a Mastiff named Hercules played a legendary ball-eating dog called "The Beast" who lives behind the baseball field. When the only baseball goes over the fence, the kids discover that The Beast is actually a friendly dog. In *The Sandlot 2*, Mastiffs Duke, a brindle male, and Susie, a fawn female, shared acting duties in the movie with Hercules as "Goliath."

For his close-up in the 2007 film, *Transformers*, Mason, the fawn Mastiff

If you are interested in adopting a Mastiff, contact the MCOA.

owned by the movie's director Michael Bay, had to actually take a bath. Bay named his dog after John Patrick Mason, Sean Connery's character in Bay's film *The Rock*.

Other Mastiffs are famous stars on the big screen, too. These include a family of Mastiffs who completed the cast of *Beethoven*, and a Mastiff who played Carlo in the 1912 movie, *The Adventures of Copper Beeches*, a Sherlock Holmes story written by Sir Arthur Conan Doyle. Hungry and protective, Carlo prowled the mansion at night to secure the Copper Beeches property.

In a 2011 TV episode of *Modern Family*, a brindle Mastiff scared backyard intruders, Claire and Mitchell, into climbing a tree house to await rescue.

Celebrity Owners

Famous people who owned Mastiffs include Charles Dickens and his dog Turk, George C. Scott, Marlon Brando, Michael Bay, Kirstie Alley, and Bob Dylan.

Art, Literature, and Collectibles

Historically, Mastiffs are an integral part of royal families, and they are represented in art, literature, and collectibles.

According to *Stowe's Annual*, a reference book, King James I (1603–1625) of England sent two Lyme Hall Mastiffs to Phillip II of Spain as a gift. Either these dogs or their descendants appear in portraits of the Spanish royal children.

Diego Velasquez, the leading Spanish artist of the 15th to 17th centuries, included Phillip IV's apricot Mastiff in his portrait *Las Meninas* in 1656, and the Flemish Baroque artist Sir Anthony van Dyck included a Mastiff in his 1637 depiction of the English royal children of Charles I of England.

James Fenimore Cooper and Alfred, Lord Tennyson, included Mastiffs in their literature, and a Mastiff is mentioned in Sir Arthur Conan Doyle's *The Hound of the Baskervilles*.

Today, like many passionate dog owners, Mastiff lovers treasure gifts and collectibles depicting Mastiffs. These range from the whimsical to the accurate renderings of the breed in all price ranges. They include jewelry, stamps, paintings, statutes, stationery, clothing, kitchen accessories, home décor, calendars, flags, signs, office supplies, memory boxes, car license plate holders, and holiday ornaments. Visit any dog show or go online and you'll find a plethora of Mastiff merchandise.

From his centuries spent as a guard dog, the Mastiff's overpowering looks often frighten people. To others more familiar with his good nature, the breed is protective, yet calm and devoted.

Chapter
2

Characteristics
of Your Mastiff

When you think about a Mastiff, one word comes to mind: massive. Picture 100 pounds (45 kg) plus. This heavy-boned, powerful dog is a vision of dignity and grandeur. Standing nearly 36 inches (91 cm) tall, this gentle giant has been bred for size, courage, and docility.

Powerful and naturally inquisitive, most Mastiffs quickly approach new objects, but are often slower to investigate new people and may even appear somewhat reserved at times. They prefer to observe first rather than jump into the fray. However, once the Mastiff bonds with his family, his loyalty is undeniable. A keen sense of humor and a calm nature set the Mastiff apart from other jumbo-size breeds.

The Mastiff's Physical Characteristics

The greatest Mastiff is probably the one resting at your feet. While he may or may not resemble the "ideal" Mastiff, he's no doubt the love of your life. Yet, if he possesses some picture-perfect characteristics, it's not by accident. Whether you want to show your dog or just live with a wonderful canine companion, conscientious breeders work hard at producing a dog with Mastiff characteristics by following a blueprint. This blueprint is the Mastiff Club of America's (MCOA) breed standard, a finely written description of what the ideal Mastiff should look and act like.

The standard outlines every aspect of the breed, from its general appearance, size, proportion, and substance to the specifics of its head, body, legs, coat, and color. It also includes the dog's gait and temperament. This unique set of characteristics defines the Mastiff's utility as a working breed.

Just as a dollar must be a precise size and shade of green and possess certain markings before you can buy anything with it, so must a Mastiff fit the breed standard to be called a Mastiff. It's what keeps the breed looking and behaving the same for generations.

Breed Type

The individual characteristics that distinguish a Mastiff from other breeds are known as breed type, or the essence of the breed. Breed type comes from the original reason the breed was developed. These traits, such as the Mastiff's size and temperament, have been carefully reproduced over generations to produce the Mastiff that is recognized today.

Height and Weight

Don't even think of leaving food unattended in the kitchen, even for an instant. A Mastiff is tall enough to rest his massive head on the countertop. In one gulp, he can devour your dinner if he really wants to.

Check It Out

MASTIFF FAST FACTS

✓ **Height**: Males—at least 30 inches (76 cm); Females—at least 27.5 inches (70 cm). Generally up to 36 inches (91 cm).

✓ **Weight**: Males—160 to 230 pounds (73 to 105 kg); Females 120 to 170 pounds (55 to 77 kg) or more.

✓ **Coat Type**: Double-coated. Outer coat straight, coarse, and medium to short. Undercoat short and dense.

✓ **Coat Colors**: Fawn, apricot, or brindle. Very little white confined to the chest or toes.

✓ **Life Expectancy**: 10 years.

Although there is no upper height limit in the Mastiff standard, it does state a minimum height requirement. Males should be at least 30 inches (76 cm) high when measured from the ground to the shoulder. Females should be at least 27.5 inches (70 cm) tall. A tall Mastiff may measure as much as 36 inches (91 cm).

The standard does not mention a weight requirement, but the Mastiff ranges from 120 to 230 pounds (54.5 to 104.5 kg). The males weigh around 160 to 230 pounds (72.7 to 104.5 kg) and females 120 to 170 pounds (54.5 to 77.3 kg). According to the MCOA, a Mastiff named Zorba, the word's largest dog, weighed 343 pounds (155.9 kg).

Coat

A Mastiff's coat is double-layered and fit for a working dog. The water-resistant outer coat and the shorter, insulating undercoat are designed to keep him warm and dry. The outer coat is moderately short, straight, and coarse.

The undercoat is short and dense. Unlike other breeds with two coats, the Mastiff's coat shouldn't grow long enough to produce fringe on the belly, tail, or hind legs. A true Mastiff coat is never long or wavy. Expect major shedding from this breed.

Colors

Mastiffs come in three colors: Fawn, apricot, or brindle—all with a black mask and ears. If there is any white, it should be confined to the chest and toes. Too much white on the chest or any other part of the body is not acceptable for showing.

The brindle coat pattern should have fawn or apricot as a background, which should be covered with very dark, irregular-looking stripes. This flecked shading is evenly distributed throughout the body and shouldn't be blotchy.

There are variations in the fawn and brindle colors. Once known as silver-fawn, the fawn varies from very light to a darker shade closer to the redder shade of apricot, or a dull grayish-brown. Brindles vary from nearly black all over with a few faint stripes, to an apricot brindle with apricot-colored stripes. A light background instead of a dark background with a few faint stripes of another color is not acceptable. Reputable breeders do not intentionally breed for unusual colors or coat types.

Head

Mastiff breeders pay close attention to the breed's head, as it is the most distinguishing characteristic. The description of the Mastiff's head comprises the largest part of the breed standard. At any angle, the head is massive. Big, broad, and flat across the

skull between the ears, the forehead is slightly curved, with head's stop between the eyes defined but not deep or shallow. The dark brown eyes should be medium-size, set wide apart, and never bulgy. The length of the muzzle to the whole head should meet the proportion of one to three. A snipey (narrow, pointed) muzzle is not desirable. The nose is broad, and the blacker the better. True to his heritage, the Mastiff's expression is alert but kindly.

Body

Slightly longer than high, the Mastiff's body is rectangular, rather than square. The broad and deep chest is well-defined and the backbone (or topline) is straight, level, and not swaybacked or roached (overly arched). The back

HOW MUCH DO MASTIFF PUPPIES WEIGH?

It depends on the puppy's individual body type. According to one breeder, at 6 months of age, one of her smaller females weighed 66 pounds (30 kg), an average-size male 97 pounds (44 kg), while a male with massive bones tipped the scales at 110 pounds (50 kg). When full-grown, the female weighed 150 pounds (68 kg), the average male 215 pounds (98 kg), and the largest male 230 pounds (105 kg).

To determine if your puppy is at the correct weight, look at his body. From a standing position, a Mastiff puppy's ribs should not be visible. When running, the outline of the rib cage should ripple slightly.

A puppy should not be overweight. His body is still developing, and excess weight adds stress to the skeletal structure and causes damage. It's better for a puppy to be slightly underweight than overweight.

Brindle is one of the breed's three colors.

should be strong and muscular, with the rump having a slight, rounded appearance.

Movement

A Mastiff should move powerfully and freely, with strength, but he is not a racer. Don't expect a Mastiff to be a jogging partner. He's not built for speed, but rather exudes power and strength while in motion.

Living With a Mastiff

Calm and gentle, the Mastiff has a way about him that lets everyone know he's in control. Before bringing this oversized caretaker into your life, consider whether you can properly return his devotion and loyalty.

Personality

In 1800, the *Cynographia Britannica,* by Sydeham Edwards, described the Mastiff with this phrase: "What the Lion is to the Cat, the Mastiff is to the Dog, the noblest

Living with a Mastiff is rewarding, but you must take his size and power into consideration.

of the family; he stands alone, and all others sink before him. His courage does not exceed his temper and generosity, and in attachment he equals the kindest of his race."

Mastiff breeders and owners say that the breed's good-natured, loyal, and docile temperament describes it perfectly. Aristocratic rather than comedic, the Mastiff rarely has a silly side. In real life, Mastiffs have a range of temperaments, and depending upon their pedigree and how they are raised, may be good-natured, mellow, or require more interaction from their owners. Often mistaken as slow or lazy, the Mastiff can move surely and swiftly when necessary.

Mastiffs can land some wet sloppy tongue baths on a guest and give a look that says, "I've got it covered," all in the same day. A well-trained and stable Mastiff serves as an excellent ambassador of the breed. Extremely intelligent and intensely emotional, they often cajole their families into doing whatever it is they want.

With a soft interior, they often push the limits during training and will remember harsh interactions. Like many breeds, they don't do well with harsh corrections. With an inexperienced dog owner, the Mastiff will often take advantage of most situations.

Companionability

Friendly and outgoing, Mastiffs crave attention from their owners. Once they do something that amuses the family, they'll repeat it. Count on a Mastiff to demand

Ask the Expert

Q: What's it like to live with a Mastiff?

A: The Mastiff has a fabulous temperament. He's the original pacifist, and has never been known as an aggressive dog. With an easy-going, gentle disposition, the Mastiff really wants to please you, but it has to be his idea.

When my Mastiff Danny would beg at the table I'd tell him, "Down." He'd look at me without moving, so I'd say, "Down or Out." He'd leave the room and go into his crate. He'd come back a few minutes later and lie down next to the table. He'd give me a look, as if to say, "I did this because I wanted to, not because you told me to."

—Dr. William R. Newman, longtime Mastiff owner, Vice-President of the Mastiff Club of America, and vice chairman of the American Kennel Club (AKC) Board of Directors

petting. Breeder Pat Flanagan Borracci says, "I have a male who, whenever I sit on the couch, stands in front of me, climbs up on one foreleg on each side of my body, and pins me down. He proceeds to lick my whole face and nibbles on my chin. If I laugh, this encourages him to keep on going."

The Drool Factor

Do you think you can live with drool? This breed's large mouth and lower lip produce saliva—lots of saliva. While all dogs drool and pant when they're about to eat or become excited, Mastiffs are droolers extraordinaire.

Adding to the moisture quotient is the way they drink water. Some Mastiffs put their faces in the water dish while they drink, then walk away and dribble water as they go. When they shake their heads, they fling drool onto walls and ceiling. Here's where keeping drool rags and paper towels in every room comes in handy

If a breeder promises you that her puppies do not drool as much as other Mastiffs, don't believe her. It's simply not true.

Oh, and expect lots of "zzz" sounds from this breed—Mastiffs snore, too!

Environment

A Mastiff doesn't need a country manor with acres of land to maintain his cheerful outlook on life. Then again, what dog wouldn't love to spend his days exploring the great outdoors alongside you and sharing your bed come nighttime? A home with a fenced yard is ideal, although he can manage with less room.

This giant working breed weighs 100

pounds (45.5 kg) or more. He needs enough space to comfortably move around in without bumping into walls and family members. Cramped quarters shrink even more once you add a dog of this size.

Glass or fragile objects must be stored up and out of your Mastiff's reach. His powerful tail can wipe out anything 2.5 feet (0.8 m) high and below. Also, think twice before allowing your Mastiff a place on the bed or couch. Once this giant dog sprawls out, you'll need your own sleeping quarters.

A Mastiff appreciates a fenced-in yard to stretch out his legs, and it will also make housetraining easier. It comes in handy to work off some excess energy, retrieve the ball a few times, and just relax. If you're dedicated to walking your dog outdoors a few times a day to potty, and you can provide daily exercise, then a condominium or large apartment without stairs might work.

This jumbo-size dog should never be left alone in a yard 24/7, regardless of how secure or ideal the space may seem.

The Mastiff requires a moderate amount of exercise, and his activity level is generally low.

Mastiffs need to live indoors, as they are terribly attached to their families and many suffer separation anxiety when isolated.

Exercise Requirements

The Mastiff requires a moderate amount of exercise, and his activity level is generally low. Like people, your Mastiff needs some daily exercise to help keep him mentally and physically fit. Exercise builds strong bones, adds muscular strength, and prevents obesity. An exercised dog is a happy dog.

Muscular and athletic, a Mastiff enjoys short walks or easy hikes on soft surfaces and the chance to get out of the house and check out the scenery. Make sure the weather is moderate, as this breed overheats easily and has a difficult time tolerating hot or cold temperatures (air doesn't flow as well through the Mastiff's flat muzzle as it does through those of other breeds). Taking your Mastiff off-lead, except in a completely enclosed area, is a bad idea. Like a runaway freight train, if your dog chooses to run off, you'll have a hard time convincing him to return.

A few minutes of chasing a ball is a good physical outlet, but don't count on a Mastiff to retrieve endlessly. After a few fetches, a Mastiff may decide that if you want the ball badly enough, you should probably go get it yourself. In addition, this is not the breed for someone looking for a jogging partner. While a Mastiff may decide to sprint now and then, it's usually on his own terms. Some Mastiffs are fascinated with water and will happily splash around in a lake or stream and cavort through sprinklers.

If you prefer organized canine performance activities, a Mastiff can participate in agility, rally obedience, tracking, drafting, or carting. This noble breed makes an excellent therapy dog, and is a willing search and rescue partner.

Around the house, a Mastiff is generally content to sit quietly at your feet or follow you from room to room. It's not unusual for a Mastiff to maintain body contact with you. Either he's leaning up against you or plopping his huge head in your lap. Sleeping and warming the couch are favorite pastimes.

Physical Limitations

As with other medium-, large-, and giant-breed puppies, Mastiffs younger than 2 years of age should never walk or run long distances. Bones are developing and can easily become injured if stressed.

How far can you walk with a Mastiff puppy? From the age of 4 to 6 months, walk one or two short blocks. By 6 to 7 months of age, walk several blocks or up to 1 mile (2 km). At 1 year, he's ready for a 2-mile (3-km) walk. Always watch for signs of fatigue—panting or slowing down. A tired pup will lie down and

Consider whether owning a giant breed will fit into your budget.

Limit unnecessary trips up and down stairs, as too much stair climbing can damage growing bones. Going down shifts the dog's weight to the front of his body and produces pounding on his shoulders, which can damage growing bones. Use a baby gate to restrict stair access, and teach your Mastiff puppy to wait for supervision and move slowly. To train your pup to safely maneuver the stairs, attach a leash to your pup's collar to help control his speed. Ask a second person to stand in front of the puppy to prevent forging ahead. Running and jumping the flight should never be allowed, as this forces uneven weight on joints. If your dog sleeps upstairs, one or two trips a day may be manageable.

To avoid injuries, restrict puppy play with older dogs. Mastiff youngsters will try to keep up with bigger dogs and can easily become overpowered. Supervise any interaction between dogs, and when you see the puppy taking on too much, end the play session. Like children, young dogs require a lot of rest while growing.

Teach children not to roughhouse with a young Mastiff. Tackling or leaning on a puppy can stress growing bones.

refuse to move, and you may not like carrying him home!

A growing Mastiff should not spend all of his time on tile floors or cement dog runs or patios, as these surfaces are too tough on legs and feet and will cause arthritis and joint pain. It may also cause hip dysplasia. Puppies and adolescent Mastiffs should not be encouraged to jump off the bed or couch, as landing on hard surfaces causes the same problems. Don't allow your puppy to run or play on slippery tile or wood flooring. Your dog can slip and slide, increasing the risk of injuring bones.

Financial Considerations

When mulling over the prospect of adding a Mastiff to your household, consider whether owning a giant breed will fit into your budget. Veterinary expenses are often higher for giant breeds, as the cost of medications and surgeries is based on weight. You'll need more dog food too, and feeding a quality diet to your dog can be costly. The price of bigger dog beds and crates, leashes, collars, and grooming supplies can be considerable, too.

The Mastiff is not some little dog you can tuck under your arm and take traveling with you. Is your car large enough to safely contain a giant dog? Don't forget the chomp factor. If he's bored or feeling neglected, a Mastiff will chew anything he can fit his mouth around, including your furniture, the wall, or his toys. Replacing these things adds up.

Trainability

Like every dog, the strong, powerful Mastiff requires training. Positive methods with early socialization encourage your dog to interact well with others. (See Chapter 6: Training Your Mastiff). Begin training as soon as you bring your dog home, and keep your sessions short. The Mastiff is an intelligent breed who catches on quickly and doesn't appreciate endless drilling.

Sociability With Children

When raised around well-behaved children, the Mastiff can be a loyal, loving companion. Generally, they are wonderful with children, but always be aware of the

size difference. Some Mastiffs love to offer a paw, which can scratch the face and hands of a small child, although it's far from intentional.

It helps if your dog has been socialized to children and feels comfortable around them, but lacking this experience, the Mastiff doesn't know what to expect. Kids are naturally boisterous, often unpredictable, and can make sudden movements that may frighten a Mastiff. When this happens, any breed can launch a fear bite if they sense a threat. Dog bites injure nearly five million people every year, with half of all kids bitten by age 12.

To prevent dog bites and to foster a safe, easy-going relationship between Mastiff and children, follow these tips.

1. Always supervise interactions. No dog, no matter how lovable or mild-mannered he seems, should ever be left alone with little ones. Accidents happen, and an adult should always be present to prevent missteps. Never allow a child to take your Mastiff out for a walk—even down the driveway—without your supervision.

2. Respect mastiff space. Instruct children not to bother your Mastiff while he's eating, sleeping, playing with a toy, or resting in his crate. Your dog needs his privacy and may become possessive with his things.

3. Ask permission. Youngsters should always ask permission before petting or offering a treat. Show them how to give the tidbit in an open, outstretched hand. When children hold the food too close to their bodies or over the dog's head, it encourages jumping up and the Mastiff can accidentally knock them over.

4. Move slowly. Sudden movements may frighten a Mastiff, and running near him may trigger a nip. Instruct children to play quietly when the dog is in the room.

5. No sitting on or hugging the dog. Many dog bites happen when children want to sit on or hug and kiss the dog. Some Mastiffs may interpret this as a threat and could bite.

6. Train your dog. Once you train your Mastiff to sit, let youngsters give your dog the sit cue for a treat. This sends the message to the dog that the child is in charge. Children should always praise the dog for a job well done and never punish him.

7. Act like a log. If your Mastiff accidentally knocks your child over, teach your little one to roll up in a ball and lie still. A frightened, moving child might encourage the dog to roughhouse or chase, which could result in injuries.

8. Don't walk around carrying food. Never let a child walk around the house with food. Your Mastiff may think the goody is for him and will

If you want a quality pet Mastiff, the best place to find one is from a responsible breeder.

try to grab it. In the process, he can accidentally injure the child's hand. Other than the occasional whack of a tail or a tumble to the floor, Mastiffs are a good choice for well-behaved children.

Sociability With Other Pets

The gentle-giant nature of the Mastiff dictates getting along with other dogs and animals. This holds true when the dog is socialized with other puppies and pets when young. Many good-tempered Mastiffs will play with small dogs. However, if a Mastiff has never been introduced to other animals, he's not trustworthy to get up close and personal with other adult dogs (especially males), cats, or smaller pets. It's not wise, either, to bring an adult Mastiff into a home that already has an adult dog of the same sex.

Buying a Mastiff Puppy

If you want a quality pet Mastiff, the best place to find one is from a breeder who shows her dogs. It doesn't mean that you have to show the puppy, and not all puppies in a show-bred litter are destined for the show ring. Many go to pet homes. A pet-quality puppy from a show-bred litter is raised with the same high

Schedule a visit to the breeder's home if you are interested in purchasing a puppy.

standards of health, temperament, and conformation as the show puppies in the same litter.

Contact the Mastiff Club of America online at www.mastiff.org for a breeder referral list (or if you want to adopt an older Mastiff). Breeders who are members of the MCOA must abide by a code of ethics regarding selling puppies. Another way to meet breeders is to go to a dog show.

To select a breeder:

1. Ask if they test their stock for genetic problems (see Chapter 9 for information on Mastiff health problems). Request to see the paperwork showing the testing results from veterinary specialists. You can also check the Canine Health Information Center's website (www.caninehealthinfo.org) to find testing results. The parents should be clear of the genetic problems. If the breeder doesn't test, inquire why.

2. Interview breeders. Ask how long a breeder has been involved with the breed. The more experience

a breeder has, the more likely she can help you if your dog ever has a problem.

3. Fill out the questionnaire. If a breeder wants to know if you can provide a good home for a Mastiff, she may ask about your lifestyle and level of dog experience. That's OK. If she doesn't show any interest in the life the puppy would lead once he leaves her home, look elsewhere.

4. Schedule a visit. See the breeder's dogs. The premises should be clean, and the puppies and adult dogs should appear healthy and in good condition.

5. Beware of "designer" Mastiffs. If a breeder advertises an "American Mastiff" as superior stock to the Mastiff, recognize that this is actually a mixed-breed dog. It's an English Mastiff crossed with an Anatolian Shepherd or another breed.

6. Look at the Sales Agreement. A conscientious Mastiff breeder should sell a puppy on a written contract. This should include care and health provisions, and require new owners to spay or neuter the dog at the appropriate age. The breeder should agree to take back any Mastiff the buyer no longer wants.

7. Make sure there's a health guarantee. A good Mastiff breeder should offer a health guarantee. Make sure you understand the terms of the guarantee. Copies of the sire and dam and puppy's health records, including vaccination and deworming history and the veterinarian's examination, should also be included.

8. Get the paperwork. Make sure the breeder gives you information about how to care for your Mastiff. The papers should include a three-generation (or more) pedigree, the American Kennel Club (AKC) registration application, and the sales agreement.

Chapter
3

Supplies for
Your Mastiff

Part of the fun in adding a Mastiff to your life involves stocking up on doggy supplies. Whether you're acquiring a new puppy or an older dog, you'll need to schedule a shopping trip. If possible, arrange to go to the store before your dog comes home. This gives you time to focus on helping your new Mastiff adjust to his new surroundings, without having to worry about searching for bargains.

Preparing for your Mastiff's arrival comes with a price tag, but fortunately the breed isn't fussy and doesn't call for specialized or fancy equipment. Your dog will need a few basics, but these will last a long time. Other items, such as collars, toys, and bedding, will require replacing from time to time. To cut your expenses, compare prices at online stores, pet supply warehouses, and small independent boutiques.

Baby or Canine Gates

Baby gates are indispensable for blocking off areas of the house that you don't want your dog to wander into. It's easier to housetrain your dog and protect your belongings from any destructive chewing if you can restrict his access to certain rooms.

Select sturdy gates that are easy for you—but not your dog—to open and

Regular-sized beds won't do for your Mastiff—buy the largest size you can find.

Check It Out

SUPPLIES CHECKLIST

Here's a list of supplies your Mastiff will need. It helps to have many of these on hand when your dog comes home. The rest you can buy as you need them.

- ✓ Anti-chew spray
- ✓ Canine nail clippers and/or electric nail grinder
- ✓ Canine oral hygiene spray or gel
- ✓ Canine rubber brush
- ✓ Canine shampoo
- ✓ Canine toothbrush and toothpaste
- ✓ Clean-up supplies, including stain and odor remover
- ✓ Collar and 6-foot (2-m) leash
- ✓ Cornstarch or styptic powder or pencil to stop nail bleeds
- ✓ Crate
- ✓ Dog bed
- ✓ Exercise pen
- ✓ Flea, tick, and heartworm preventives
- ✓ Food
- ✓ Food and water bowls
- ✓ Food storage bin
- ✓ Hand-held shower sprayer
- ✓ Identification (ID tag and microchip)
- ✓ Large towels or pet hair dryer
- ✓ Medicated ear cleaner and cotton strips
- ✓ Non-slip rubber mat for bathing
- ✓ Pet or child gate
- ✓ Pet seat belt
- ✓ Safe toys and chews
- ✓ Trash containers with lids

close. Gates with vertical bars will discourage your Mastiff from climbing up and over the boundary.

Bed

While a crate with a soft pad and a blanket can double as a bed, your Mastiff will appreciate kicking back in a cushy pillow-bed in another room in the house. You'll need the largest size you can find so your dog can stretch out, but hold off purchasing one until he's over the chewing stage.

Cleaning Supplies

Add an enzymatic carpet cleaner to your list of must-have dog supplies. This destroys the odor-causing molecules in canine eliminations and discourages your dog from returning to the same indoor potty spot.

A pooper-scoop for yard cleanup proves indispensable for Mastiff-size eliminations. Or, consider an in-ground pet waste disposal system. This miniature septic tank is environmentally friendly as it reduces waste to a ground-absorbed liquid. Don't forget to purchase

Choose a sturdy collar for your Mastiff.

biodegradable poop bags to take on outings with your dog.

Collar

If you're purchasing a Mastiff puppy, ask your breeder what size collar will fit. Or, carry your pup into the store with you and try a few collars on him. A good fit for a puppy or an adult dog allows you to slide two fingers between the collar and your dog's neck.

Resist the urge to purchase a collar that's too big now, thinking that your dog will grow into it. A collar that's too big serves no purpose and will only fall off or possibly catch on objects. Plan on purchasing several different sized collars until your Mastiff is fully grown.

You'll find collars ranging in price from expensive custom types to economical, but a simple design works well. Choose one or two sturdy collars in leather, mesh, nylon, or recycled material. An extra collar always comes in handy in case the first one breaks.

PUPPY-PROOFING

Before bringing your Mastiff home, remove anything inside your home and in the yard that he's likely to discover and destroy. A Mastiff pup loves to chew and can quickly ruin your possessions. Check your floors, furniture, and tabletops for shoes, clothing, books, wallets, cell phones, computers, and pillows lying around, and put them out of your dog's reach. Hide electrical cords and pick up children's toys and small objects. If a dog swallows a foreign object, it may cause life-threatening injuries.

Prevent your dog from getting into the kitchen or garage trash with a tight-fitting lid he can't open. To lessen the allure of garbage, don't leave leftover food in the trash, and place kitchen and bathroom containers inside a cabinet. A Mastiff can open a cabinet with his paws so it doesn't hurt to install a child-proof latch.

Don't forget to check the garage for any sharp tools or poisonous garden or auto supplies. A Mastiff is tall enough to jump up on a work bench and grab something dangerous. Store tree pruners and power tools in locked cabinets. Relocate fertilizers, cocoa mulch, bone meal, insecticides, and antifreeze out of your dog's reach, as these are poisonous to dogs.

Contact the ASPCA's Animal Poison Control Center (888-426-4435) if you suspect that your Mastiff may have eaten something poisonous in your home or yard. There is a consultation fee for this service. For a list of toxic and non-toxic plants, check their website at www.aspca.org/pet-care/poison-control.

Crate

Don't think of a crate as a jail. It's actually a training tool to housetrain your puppy, a cozy place for him to catch some zzz's, and a safe retreat from rambunctious children. Crates are available in wire, which work well for Mastiffs as wire crates provide good ventilation, fold flat, and transport easily; plastic, which are approved for airline shipping and provide protection from drafts; and soft-sided fabric, although these are not recommended unless you can supervise their use. A Mastiff can easily chew a hole through the sides if he wants out badly enough.

The right size for an adult Mastiff is the

giant model, which is about 48 inches (122 cm) long, 30 to 32 inches (76 to 81 cm) wide, and 33 to 35 inches (84 to 89 cm) high. An adult dog should be able to stand up, turn around, and lie down comfortably. If you have a puppy, use a box to block off the back to make the crate smaller for him, which will aid in housetraining. In a short time, your puppy will grow into the large-size crate, so you only need to buy one crate.

Exercise Pen

Some Mastiff owners prefer using an exercise pen to a crate inside the house. It's roomier, and puppies are less likely to put up a fuss because they can see out. Anchor the pen to the floorboards to prevent the pup from scooting the pen around. An adult Mastiff who has not been raised in a pen can easily knock it over. Add a top to the pen to prevent your dog from jumping up on the sides.

Take the pen along on trips to provide a portable yard for your dog, but never leave him in an exercise pen outdoors unattended. Choose a 10-panel pen that's 5 feet (2 m) high.

Fencing

A Mastiff will appreciate cavorting inside a safe, fenced-in yard. Don't rely on electronic fencing. If a dog or an intruder enters the yard, your Mastiff is likely to chase them through the boundary and

out of the yard, despite the electric shock. And if he tries to come back into the yard, he'll receive a shock again. Your dog should never be chained up outside or left unattended on a tie-out cable either, as he can easily become injured.

Your fenced-in yard must be escape-proof, without any dangerous objects, and the gates should be firmly latched at all times. To deter your dog from jumping over the top or strangers from easily hopping into your yard, the fence should be at least 5 feet (2 m) high. Ideally, you'll be able to just open the back door to let your dog out into the yard without having to walk him on a leash to the space.

Flea, Tick, and Heartworm Preventives

When you take your new Mastiff to the veterinarian for his first check-up, discuss parasite control. To remain healthy, your dog will need to remain free from external parasites. Many parasite control products are available from your veterinarian, or you can try natural remedies to deter fleas and ticks. Some areas of the country present more of a parasite problem than others. (See Chapter 9 for more information about parasites.)

Food

If you're buying a puppy, ask his breeder what your puppy has been eating.

Ask the Expert

ELEVATED FEEDER STATION—YES OR NO?

For a Mastiff who flips his bowl or chases it all over the floor, the raised feeder is a neater solution. Then again, eating from a feeder can become a bigger mess when your Mastiff gets food stuck in his jowls, and it drops out of his mouth and falls all over everything.

I've had Mastiffs who prefer lying down on the floor to eat, dogs who stood and leaned down to a bowl on the floor, and others who dined and drank water from a raised station. It doesn't seem to make a difference. I have noticed that some dogs eat faster than others, and a fast eater seems to gulp less from a raised station.

I think feeding a dog in whatever way he eats slowly and comfortably works best.

—Pat Flanagan Borracci, breeder of Dunkirk Mastiffs, Mastiff Club of America member, and president of the Empire State Mastiff Fanciers

Chances are the breeder may even send some of the food home with you. If not, purchase the same brand at the store. Keep your dog on the same type of food for the first week or so. This gives him time to settle into your routine without having to deal with a new diet, too. If you decide to change to a different commercial recipe, or to feed your dog a homemade or a raw diet, gradually mix the new diet in with the original food to avoid stomach upset.

You'll find many types of dog food available, including recipes formulated for large-breed puppies and dogs. (See Chapter 4 for choosing the right food for your Mastiff.) Many breeders recommend feeding commercial puppy food only for

the first few months, so be prepared to change diets again, later on.

Food Storage Bin

If you're feeding your dog a high-quality dry food, you'll need to store it safely away from your dog, bugs, and rodents. Oxygen, heat, humidity, and light can damage food. To reduce environmental exposure, store an open bag of food in the bag inside of a container that has a tight-fitting lid designed for food storage.

Food and Water Bowls

Your dog needs separate bowls for food and water. Stainless steel lasts forever, is dishwasher safe, and easy to clean. Plastic and ceramic are less expensive, but will chip, and leftover bits of food can become imbedded in cracks and spoil. Choose deep 4 to 5 quart (liter) bowls for your Mastiff.

Optional Food and Water Supplies

Some Mastiff breeders use an elevated food and water feeder. This type of feeding station raises a dog's food and water bowls to his standing height, and eliminates the need to for your dog to bend down to eat or drink, thus reducing strain to the neck, back, and joints.

While an elevated feeding station may prove beneficial to senior or arthritic dogs who have difficulty bending over, it may not be the best choice for large-breed dogs like Mastiffs, who are susceptible to gastric dilatation volvulus (GDV). This extremely serious disorder, commonly called "bloat" or "stomach torsion," occurs when the dog's stomach fills with air and becomes twisted, and it can be life-threatening. A study published in the *Journal of American Veterinary Medical Association* in 2000 reported that elevated feeders actually increase the risks of bloat by 110%. If you do decide to use a raised feeding station, it should reach your Mastiff's chest—about 12 to 16 inches (30 to 41 cm) high from the floor.

Some Mastiff breeders like to install an automatic water attachment to their outdoor hose faucet. By licking it, the dog controls the flow of water he drinks to a slow and continuous trickle. This prevents guzzling a large amount of water, which may cause bloat.

Grooming Supplies

To keep your Mastiff's skin and coat in tip-top shape, you'll need a rubber brush. Don't use a bristle brush, as it will tear the coat. Purchase a shampoo that's formulated for dogs, rather than people, as human shampoo has a higher pH that's harsh on a dog's skin and coat. If your dog has skin issues, choose an oatmeal-based or hypoallergenic formula. A natural dog shampoo, rather than a chemical-based dog soap, contains organic herbs, antioxidants, and moisturizers that condition the coat and prevent skin irritation.

You won't need a fancy bathtub to bathe a Mastiff. On a warm day, wash him off outdoors with a bucket and some warm water. In cooler weather, a roomy stall shower that's easy for him to walk in and out of makes an ideal spa location. Use a large rubber bath mat inside the shower and a large towel on the bathroom floor to prevent your dog from slipping. To make rinsing off the soap easier, it helps to have a hand-held shower sprayer attachment. You'll need several extra-large towels to adequately dry your dog, or invest in a canine hair dryer to save time and laundry. This product uses a cooler setting than a human hair dryer, thus avoiding damage to the coat or burning the skin.

Clipping your dog's nails once a week helps maintain his feet in good condition. Choose between two types of doggy nail clippers: guillotine or scissors style to remove the tips of the nails. For an even closer trim, use an electric nail grinder. (See Chapter 5 for tips to help groom your dog.)

Don't forget a canine toothbrush, which is angled to fit a dog's mouth more comfortably than a human toothbrush. You'll also need canine toothpaste. Available in several flavors, it's formulated for dogs and doesn't require rinsing. Besides, dogs love the taste of doggy toothpaste! In addition to brushing, a canine oral hygiene spray or gel, available from your veterinarian, will help reduce bacteria, which lead to gingivitis and dental decay.

Mastiff ears need regular cleaning. Ask your veterinarian for a good ear cleaner for your dog or use mineral oil to loosen ear wax. Long strips of absorbent cotton work best to remove debris. Don't use cotton applicators, cotton balls, baby wipes, or makeup remover pads, as these may harm your dog's ears, may not reach into the ear far enough to remove debris, or could contain harmful chemicals.

Identification

Securely attach an identification tag to your Mastiff's collar with a sturdy split ring. Engrave the tag with his name, your name, address, and phone number. It doesn't hurt to have a duplicate tag in case the first one becomes lost. You can even attach a nameplate directly to your dog's collar.

If your Mastiff ever becomes lost and his collar and ID tag fall off, a silicon microchip, also called a transponder, can help reunite you. About the size of a grain

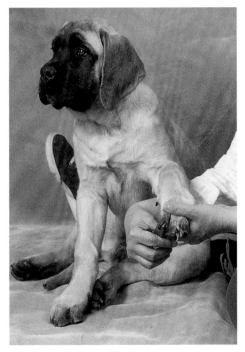

Clipping your dog's nails once a week helps maintain his feet in good condition.

of rice, your veterinarian can painlessly insert the chip at the top of your dog's shoulders, beneath the skin. It contains your contact information, which is stored in a central database. By passing a special hand-held scanner over your dog, a shelter can detect this information and notify you.

If you're traveling with your dog or like to take him for long walks, consider attaching a canine global positioning system onto your dog's collar for extra protection.

Leash

Your dog will need a leash whenever you take him outside for exercise or car rides. Purchase one or two sturdy 6-foot (2-m) leather leashes, 3/4- or 1-inch (2- or 3-cm) wide. These are strong enough for a Mastiff, and a back-up leash always comes in handy. While nylon is less expensive, it's hard on your hands when a Mastiff decides to lunge. Keep a leather leash out of your dog's mouth when you're not walking him and it will last a lifetime.

Skip purchasing a retractable cord leash that automatically extends when you release a button, as special precautions must be taken with this leash. Once your dog ventures out more than about 6 feet (2 m), you'll have no control if he encounters an aggressive dog or traffic. Reeling in a Mastiff on a moment's

Puppy Love

GIVING NIGHTTIME COMFORT

When your new Mastiff pup lived in his former home, he slept with his littermates. Now without his siblings to cuddle up against at night, he may feel lonely. The first few days and nights in a new home can be scary. To ease the separation, give your dog a large pet plush toy to bunk with in his crate. Sure, he knows it's not a live dog, but it's a soft replacement. Add one or two chew toys, a blanket, and an article of your clothing carrying your scent. These will help reassure him that he's not alone. If he awakens during the night, whisper encouraging words to comfort him and he should settle down.

Place his crate next to your bed. Knowing that you are close by when the lights go out lets him know that he's not abandoned. Confined to this area, he won't potty where he sleeps. If a crate doesn't fit in your bedroom, put a blanket or a soft dog bed on the floor alongside your bed and let him sleep there. Clip his leash onto the bed frame so he's not tempted to jump on the bed or wander out of the room. Or, let him sleep in a child's playpen set up next to your bed.

notice can prove difficult. Some people experience difficulty holding onto the handle, and a dog can easily jerk the leash out of your hand and take off running. If the cord runs across human skin, it can cause a severe cut.

Toys and Chews

With their powerful jaws, Mastiff youngsters are serious chewers with a raging need to chew. As baby teeth erupt and begin to fall out, chewing helps ease teething pain. Keep a good supply of sturdy toys on hand to prevent your Mastiff from using your furniture and household objects as chew toys. Buy the biggest and sturdiest ones you can find. Anything you give your dog shouldn't be small enough to swallow or remain hidden in his mouth. Choose playthings without small pieces, such as bells or squeakers, that may break off and become lodged in the throat. These can cause major intestinal damage if your dog ingests them.

Your dog will like large rope toys, Nylabones, or large, raw beef bones.

Mastiffs are serious chewers, so purchase durable and safe chews.

Never give your dog cooked bones as these will splinter and cause choking. Edible chews or breath fresheners offer another chewing alternative. While they don't last long, they offer your dog short-time amusement.

Avoid giving your dog tennis balls or baseballs to chomp. A Mastiff will chew off the top layers and swallow them. If you want to entertain your dog with a ball, choose a soccer or basketball. Many Mastiffs enjoy nudging along and chasing after a human fitness ball or an oversized hard plastic ball. An old tire or 5-gallon water bottle make good toys, too. Just remember to monitor your dog while he's playing with his toys. If you see him beginning to tear pieces off an object, it's time to remove it.

Chapter
4

Feeding Your Mastiff

Grill a steak dinner for the family and your Mastiff will drool a small pool on your kitchen floor. The aroma pushes his strong sense of smell into overdrive. Give him a bowlful of cold kibble and don't be surprised if he gives it a sniff, turns his nose up, and walks away. Some Mastiffs can be picky eaters, but this doesn't mean that you should give him table scraps to get him to eat. Others Mastiffs are chow hounds—make that chow working dogs—and they will eat anything you put before them.

Choosy or not, your Mastiff requires good nutrition to keep his giant physique in healthy condition. Dogs are omnivores, meaning that they can eat a wide variety of foods. Integrating a wholesome combination of six different nutrients in the right amount and ratio into your dog's meals provides ideal health. He'll need a well-balanced diet containing proteins, carbohydrates, fats, vitamins and minerals, and water.

Choosing what brand or type of food to serve your Mastiff can be confusing. Today, manufacturers offer a wide range of dry, dehydrated, semi-moist, or canned choices, all containing a range of ingredients. You can also opt for cooking your own dog food or serving up a bones and raw food diet. Treats are an integral part of your dog's daily regimen, too, and you'll encounter goodies in many varieties.

No single food or ingredient works for all dogs. Some Mastiffs are picky eaters, others wolf down everything, and yet another group does not think of mealtime as their life's goal. Every Mastiff loves a treat and a hug and can be motivated to please you with enough praise and a special goody.

Some dogs can tolerate any type of diet, while others may have allergies to certain ingredients, such as beef, chicken, or grain. As dogs age, their nutritional needs change so you'll need to reevaluate the food as time goes on. Every Mastiff's needs are different depending on his age, environment, activity, health, and level of emotional or physical stress. A Mastiff who hangs around the house all day requires fewer calories than a Mastiff who guards a flock every day. Generally, a Mastiff puppy can eat between 8 and 12 cups of food daily, and an adult requires about 8 cups a day.

Decide what diet makes your Mastiff look and act healthy and what fits your time and budget. Most importantly, your dog should enjoy eating the food you feed him.

Basic Nutrition

A well-balanced diet contains the following nutrients.

Carbohydrates

Carbohydrates provide a source of energy and dietary fiber. Soluble carbohydrates

FEEDING A PUPPY

Q: What do you feed a puppy?

A: Puppies benefit from a quality commercial diet containing 26 to 28 percent protein with 14 percent fat and 3 to 4 percent fiber. A recipe containing lamb and rice, or one that is grain-free with some sweet potato, works. Don't feed more than 28 percent protein and 14 percent fat. Change to an adult recipe with 23 percent protein and 12 percent fat when the puppy is four months old.

—Margo Lauritsen, 25-year breeder of Lamars Mastiffs and member of the Mastiff Club of America (MCOA) and the Redwood Empire and Empire State Mastiff clubs of New York

are easily digestible and consist of starches and sugars, while insoluble carbohydrates are more complex to digest.

Many commercial brands use grain byproducts, such as brewer's rice, corn, and wheat as fillers. These can amount to 60 percent of the total ingredients, but are lower-quality sources of carbohydrates. Their high sugar content interferes with digestion, but dog food manufacturers use them because they are inexpensive.

Better sources of carbohydrates include sweet potatoes, vegetables, and complex carbohydrates, such as barley, brown rice, oatmeal, oat bran, and quinoa. These cause fewer allergies than corn and wheat.

Fats

Fats enhance the flavor of food and provide energy more efficiently than carbohydrates. Up to 95 percent of fats can be digested and used, but like excess carbohydrates, too much fat produces excess calories and unwanted pounds (kg). On the other hand, not enough fat produces an oily or dry and flaky coat, weight loss, and slow healing of wounds.

Fats help process fat-soluble vitamins, increase the palatability of foods, and promote healthy skin and hair.

Proteins

Proteins contain 23 chemical compounds known as amino acids. A diet must provide 10 of these for proper growth and development. Proteins enable the body to convert food into energy and are the basis for many organs, muscles, bones, blood, tissues, nails, and the immune system.

Sources of protein include meats,

Vitamins

Vitamins are divided into two groups: fat-soluble (vitamins A, D, E, and K), which are stored in the body, and water-soluble (B-complex and C vitamins), which are not stored in the body and must be replaced by diet.

Vitamin C is a powerful antioxidant that can boost the immune system, stimulate wound

Fish is an excellent source of protein for your Mastiff.

poultry, fish, eggs, and dairy products. To determine if your dog is getting enough protein, look at his body and overall condition. A thin, dry coat and underdeveloped muscles may signal too little protein. For dogs who produce kidney stones or have liver or kidney problems, your veterinarian may recommend limiting the amount and type of protein. Some Mastiff breeders don't believe in feeding chicken to their dogs, as it may worsen the symptoms of dogs who have cystinuria, an inherited metabolic disorder that causes stones to form in the kidneys and urinary tract (for more information see Chapter 9: Health of Your Mastiff).

repair, and reduce the risk of cataracts. Many veterinarians believe that dogs naturally produce enough vitamin C from glucose and, unlike people, they do not require extra in their diet. Many holistic veterinarians advocate supplementing with Ester C as it helps deter some bone issues, viral diseases, and skin problems.

A good balance of vitamins in the right combinations and amounts serves your Mastiff the best. Too much or too little of any vitamin can produce an imbalance that may result in problems including anemia, eye disease, anorexia, bleeding, and bone deformities like rickets. Always consult your veterinarian before adding vitamin supplements to your dog's diet.

Minerals

Minerals are essential to the body by building bone and cartilage, transporting oxygen in the blood, producing hormones, and regulating the functioning of nerves and muscles. Minerals include calcium, phosphorus, magnesium, potassium, sodium, chloride, sulfur, and the trace minerals copper, iodine, iron, manganese, selenium, and zinc.

The right balance of minerals is important. For example, too much copper can cause liver damage in dogs who cannot normally excrete it, an extra supply of phosphorus can be harmful to dogs with kidney disease, and excess calcium can damage the skeletal system.

Supplements

If you're feeding your dog a balanced diet, chances are you won't need to add anything special. However, sometimes your dog may need a little boost from a particular supplement. Here are a few:

- Essential fatty acids (EFAs) help maintain a healthy coat and aid in reproduction and kidney functioning. Many quality commercial dog foods contain omega-3 fatty acids as these also help reduce inflammation. Omega-3 fatty acids often alleviate symptoms of arthritis, ear infections, allergies, and kidney and heart disease. Fatty acids, such as chicken fat or

salmon, fish, or safflower oil, also help produce a healthy coat and skin.
- Chondroitin sulfate and glucosamine are sometimes added to quality commercial recipes. Also available as separate supplements, these often help treat osteoarthritis.
- Coenzyme Q10 (CoQ10) is a potent antioxidant that helps protect healthy cells. It supports heart and immune function and promotes healthy gum tissue, skin, and coat.
- Digestive enzymes help break down food and increase absorption of vitamins, minerals, and fatty acids.

Fresh water and a clean bowl should always be available to your Mastiff.

FEEDING CHECKLIST

✓ Choose what type of food to feed—commercial, home-cooked, or raw diet.
✓ Evaluate ingredients and ratios on commercial dog food.
✓ Provide fresh, filtered water daily.
✓ Consider supplements if necessary.

✓ Give healthy treats.
✓ Feed twice a day.
✓ Introduce a new food gradually.
✓ Don't allow begging from the table.
✓ Give healthy portions to prevent obesity.

• Green-food supplement contains alfalfa, barley grass, blue-green algae, kelp, spirulina, and wheat grass—phytonutrients and powerful antioxidants.

Water

Of all the nutrients, water is the most important. Since 60 percent of a dog's body is water, losing only 10 percent of it can jeopardize health. To remain hydrated, your Mastiff needs to drink approximately 1/4 cup (60 ml) of water per 2.2 pounds (1 kg) of his weight per day. For a 160-pound (73-kg) Mastiff this means drinking about 18.5 cups (4.4 l) of water a day. If the weather is hot or your dog is exercising, he'll need to drink at least two or three times that amount.

Mastiff puppies drink a lot of water, and this habit continues throughout adulthood. A clean bowl of fresh bottled spring, distilled, or filtered tap water is best. Household tap water contains chemical additives, such as chlorine and fluoride, with a high concentration of nitrates, iron, and magnesium that your dog doesn't need. To give your dog filtered tap water, many economical ways are available.

Fresh water and a clean bowl should always be available. Drool accumulates at the bottom of the water dish, and most Mastiffs will not drink the water if it contains foreign particles, drool included. While an outdoor automatic refilling water bowl may seem like a good idea for a Mastiff because it provides consistent fresh water at all times, you'll still need to thoroughly scrub the bowl out every day. If you wouldn't drink your dog's water, don't expect him to either.

Food Choices

One look at a Mastiff and it's easy to imagine feeding him large quantities of food—but it's not how much he eats, but rather what he eats that matters. From

Make sure your Mastiff puppy is getting the right balance of nutrients.

home-prepared foods to several types of commercial diets available—dry, dehydrated, semi-moist, and canned—there are more ways to feed your dog than ever before. A good diet for a Mastiff depends on feeding the right ingredients for his size and activity level and what he likes to eat.

Commercial Food

A lot of research by veterinarians and food manufacturers has gone into canine nutrition and what constitutes a healthy meal for dogs in different stages of life.

Nutritional ratios are specifically geared for puppies, adult dogs of all sizes and activity levels, pregnant females, and senior dogs.

Food advertisers also invest millions of dollars to produce expensive television and print ads and attractive packaging to convince owners to purchase their products. Dog food is, after all, a highly competitive market.

When choosing the right food for your Mastiff, it's not the one that's least expensive or most advertised that's necessarily the best for your dog.

DOG FOOD LABELS

Before buying a bag or a can of dog food, read the label on the package. It should have the words "complete and balanced." This means that the recipe meets the nutritional standards established by the American Association of Feed Control Officials (AAFCO) and based on regulations from the Food and Drug Administration (FDA), U.S. Department of Agriculture (USDA), and Federal Trade Commission (FTC) for canine adults, seniors, puppies, and pregnant females.

All ingredients in a commercial food must be listed according to percentage weight, from highest to lowest. Quality foods contain whole, higher-quality ingredients rather than byproducts, while less expensive foods use cheaper ingredients. This requires dogs to consume more of the inferior food to obtain enough nutrition.

Look for a food that lists a meat protein as the first ingredient on the label. That protein should be a whole meat (chicken, turkey, beef, lamb, fish) rather than meat byproducts. Avoid byproducts as these include the lungs, kidneys, brain, and intestines, which are inferior protein sources. The words "meat meal" actually translate to rendered animal tissues, which could include hide trimmings, hair, feathers, or hooves.

Dry Food

When you think about how much a Mastiff eats, nothing seems more convenient than opening a bag of dog food and pouring some into the bowl. Dry dog food, also called kibble, is cost effective, can be purchased in large quantities, stores easily, and doesn't require refrigeration.

Dry food comes in a variety of ingredients and ratios geared for different life stages, such as puppy, adult, and senior, but not every bag of kibble is created equal. Inferior foods are high in fats and refined carbohydrates that contribute to obesity.

Also, many inferior foods contain one or more of these nine ingredients that you should avoid feeding to your dog:

1. **Butylated hydroxyanisole (BHA) and butylated hydroxytoluene (BHT):** Some studies report that these preservatives are carcinogenic. Premium foods use ascorbate and vitamin E (mixed tocopherols) as preservatives.

2. **Ethoxyquin:** A chemically synthesized preservative. Some reports link this to impaired liver and kidney function.

3. **Propylene glycol**: A liquid used to prevent drying out, but it may affect kidney function.

4. **Propyl gallate**: A powder antioxidant that prevents fats and oils from spoiling. Has been known to cause stomach and skin irritations in people.

5. **Coloring agents**: Red 40 and Yellow 5 enhance the appearance of food, which is an unnecessary additive.

6. **Phosphoric acid**: A clear liquid used as an emulsifier and flavoring agent to prevent discoloration. This can irritate the skin and mucous membranes.

7. **Sorbitol**: A sugar substitute used to flavor food. In large quantities, it causes diarrhea and intestinal upset.

8. **Dl-alpha tocopheryl acetate**: A synthetic form of vitamin E not absorbed as easily as mixed tocopherols. Natural dog food uses vitamin E as a preservative.

9. **Menadione sodium bisulfite (vitamin K3)**: A synthetic of vitamin K that can irritate mucous membranes.

Look for a premium food that avoids using these kinds of ingredients. (The box "Dog Food Labels" has a list of what to look for in a premium dog food.) Many premium recipes include healthy supplements, such as glucosamine and chondroitin, and essential fatty acids. A growing number of Mastiff breeders and owners feed their dogs a premium dog

Containing more meat and fat than kibble, canned food is easy to digest.

food and add healthy human leftovers to the food bowl. These include fresh, raw, or lightlysteamed vegetables and diced fresh fruits, baked or steamed sweet potatoes, oatmeal, rice, cottage cheese, plain yogurt, or eggs. If you don't give them to your dog directly from the table, he won't hang around and beg.

Dehydrated Food

A fairly new type of food available for dogs comes in a dehydrated form made with human-grade ingredients. A natural alternative to dry food, dehydrated food contains fresh meats, grains, and vegetables. It is prepared by dehydration at low temperatures, which retains natural nutrients. Regular dry food is manufactured by cooking at high heat, which loses many nutrients. To serve a dehydrated food, it must be combined with warm water to yield a moist meal.

Semi-Moist Food

An expensive but tasty way to give a giant-breed dog a treat during training, semi-moist food doesn't require refrigeration and comes packaged in individual serving packets. To satisfy a Mastiff, you would need to feed several portions per meal, so it may not be the best choice. Another disadvantage to feeding semi-moist to a Mastiff is that it contains corn syrup, which tends to make dogs thirsty and increases the chances of obesity and dental issues.

Canned Food

Despite the fact that canned food contains mostly water—about 75 percent—it has a strong aroma that most dogs drool over. Containing more meat and fat than kibble, canned food is easy to digest. Following a surgery and while returning to a solid food, a few tablespoons of canned food often helps to perk up a recuperating Mastiff. An expensive option, canned food has fewer nutrients than a good kibble. Your dog has to eat more of it to receive enough nutrition.

Noncommercial Meal Options

When particular brands of commercial pet food tainted with melamine threatened dogs' lives in 2007, many owners paid more attention to reading the list of ingredients on the labels. They realized that what they put into their dog's food bowl affected the quality of their dog's health, and they turned to alternative ways to feed their dogs.

Today, more dog owners than ever before are looking at the best way to feed their dogs. In 2009, pet owners in the United States bought 24 percent more natural and organic pet food than they did only two years before. Others decided to forgo commercial diets altogether.

Some dog owners prefer to give their dogs a fresh, home-cooked or raw food diet because it avoids the artificial preservatives and byproducts present in many commercial recipes. They believe that feeding all-natural foods emulates what dogs originally ate in the wild and is a healthier way to eat. But, although dogs love the aroma and taste of whole foods with quality ingredients, the meal needs to contain the correct proportion of protein, fats, carbohydrates, vitamins, and minerals to provide good nutrition.

Going noncommercial does not mean throwing just anything in your dog's food bowl. In general, don't feed you Mastiff junk food; candy; items containing artificial ingredients; high amounts of fat, salt, or artificial sweeteners; or cooked bones.

For more information on cooking balanced and complete meals for your

Dogs who suffer from allergies or arthritis may benefit from eating a quality, nutritious diet.

themselves. They cook up a big batch that will last for 3 or 4 days and perhaps freeze another batch. They prepare meals without any cooked bones, fried food, sauces, or other ingredients that are dangerous if dogs consume them.

A few advantages to cooking for your Mastiff include knowing exactly what ingredients he's eating, not having to use preservatives or artificial flavors or colors, and the ability to customize it to your dog's particular needs.

When cooking your own dog food, it should be a complete and balanced meal that provides the proper ratio of nutrients. It should include 30 to 60 percent protein, consisting of fresh-cooked lean chicken, turkey, duck, beef, lamb, venison, pork, or fish. Many Mastiff breeders avoid feeding chicken and turkey, as they are high in cystines and can make the symptoms worse for dogs with cystinuria (see Chapter 9 for more information).

Thirty to 60 percent should include carbohydrates in the form of cooked grains, such as rice, millet, and barley. Other options are potatoes, rolled oats, winter squash, and whole-grain bread. Ten to 30 percent of the meal should contain pureed, steamed, or diced vegetables and fruits. Include 1 percent calcium, 0.8 percent phosphorus supplements, and 8 percent or less fat, such as salmon oil, flax, borage, or canola or olive oil.

dog, contact the University of California, Davis, School of Veterinary Medicine's nutrition consultation service at 530-752-1393; or check out balanceit.com or petdiets.com

Home-Cooked Diet

Making your own dog food is not as complicated as it sounds, and it doesn't mean spending hours in the kitchen. Many Mastiff breeders prepare a balanced diet from the foods they make for

LARGE-BREED PUPPY FORMULA

Puppy food contains higher amounts of protein than does adult food. Many Mastiff breeders recommend feeding large-breed puppy food recipes only for the first four months of a Mastiff pup's life. Here's why: Studies have shown that feeding large- and giant-breed puppies too much protein after four months of age can cause their bones to grow faster than their muscles. This may lead to certain skeletal problems, such as hip dysplasia, panosteitis, and osteochondritis desiccans (OCD) (see Chapter 9 for more information). Also, puppies from seven weeks to three months need three to four meals a day.

Bones and Raw Food Diet (BARF)

The biologically appropriate raw foods diet created by Dr. Ian Billinghurst uses raw meaty bones, some vegetables, and a few carbohydrates. The raw meaty bones include chicken and turkey necks, backs, and wings. (Never give your dog cooked bones as these can splinter and cause intestinal damage.) There are pros and cons to this regimen.

Proponents of this diet claim that dogs who are fed these ingredients never need their teeth cleaned, have more energy, experience fewer skin problems, and have less chance of bloating. Critics say that raw bones cause choking, broken teeth, and intestinal blockages and perforations. Raw meat and eggs pose a threat of bacterial contamination, and special care must be taken during storage and preparation. Buying fresh, organic, certified raw meat raised without antibiotics or hormones is a healthy option. Keep it refrigerated and disinfect all food utensils after handling raw meat or eggs.

Dogs who suffer from allergies or arthritis may do well on a BARF diet, although some dogs have difficulty tolerating this meal. Others may take one sniff at raw bones filling their food bowl and reject it because of the unfamiliar aroma, texture, and temperature.

If you decide to feed a raw diet, incorporate it slowly into your dog's regular meal. Try warming it up slightly or serving at room temperature rather than right out of the refrigerator.

Treats

Whether used as a training aid or just because your Mastiff looks cute, special tidbits should be given in moderation. They should also contain the same quality

Although a Mastiff puppy needs several high-quality meals a day to aid in his growth, he doesn't need food available 24/7.

nutrition as your dog's regular diet. Look at the ingredients on the label before buying: Many treats contain artificial ingredients and contain high amounts of salt, sugar, protein, grain, and calories.

Feeding Schedule

Although a Mastiff puppy needs several high-quality meals a day to aid in his growth, he doesn't need food available 24/7—and neither does your adult dog for that matter. Free-feeding, or leaving a full bowl of food out all day, isn't necessary and actually causes problems. If you leave food out all the time and your dog picks

at his food, it's difficult to know why. Is it because he doesn't like it? Or isn't he hungry, or is he tired? Plus, if other dogs live together and share the food bowl, there's no way of knowing how much each dog is eating. Some Mastiffs will free-feed themselves right into obesity.

Instead of supplying a never-empty bowl, feed your dog a measured amount at two scheduled times—usually breakfast and dinner. Having a set feeding schedule makes housetraining a puppy easier, because you'll have a better idea of when he needs to eliminate. Plus, you'll know exactly how much your dog is getting if you have to increase or decrease his portion. You can even use a scheduled feeding time as a training opportunity—before placing the bowl down, ask your Mastiff to "sit."

For a picky eater, give your dog 15 to 20 minutes to eat. If he walks away without finishing, pick up the bowl. It's best to discard the uneaten food as it may spoil if left for the next feeding. For the second meal, fill the bowl with the other half of the day's food. Don't double-fill the bowl.

If he eats a little, then leaves, give him 15 to 20 minutes before removing the meal. Don't mix anything extra into the food to get him to eat or fill him up with treats throughout the day. Maintain this schedule and, after a few meals, he'll figure out that the cafeteria isn't open all the time.

Obesity

Canine obesity has become a major health problem, with 25 to 50 percent of all dogs, including Mastiffs, weighing

Canine obesity has become a major health problem.

far more than they should. This leads to numerous health problems, including a shorter lifespan, diabetes, bone and joint diseases, heart and lung diseases, urinary and reproductive disorders, skin conditions, and various types of cancer.

You can tell whether your Mastiff puppy is at a healthy weight by observing his body. Stand over him and look down at his body. You should be able to see the outline of his last two ribs and a curve at the waist. In an adult dog, you should be able to easily feel his ribs, but not see them sticking out. If you can clearly see your dog's spine protruding upward, he's probably underweight.

To change your dog's weight, you don't need to feed him any special diet. Just make a few changes gradually. If he needs to lose weight, increase his exercise by adding a few minutes each day and decrease his food intake by 1/4 to 1/2 cup at each meal. To put on a few pounds, lighten up on the workouts and add 1/4 to 1/2 cup of food extra at each meal. It's possible that a weight gain may signal a medical problem, so always check with your veterinarian before putting your dog on a diet.

Avoid These Foods

While an occasional tiny piece of chocolate may not hurt your dog, swallowing about 50 to 100 milligrams per pound may be lethal. Other dangerous foods include coffee beans or grounds, sugar-free candy or gum containing the artificial sweetener xylitol, onions, macadamia nuts, raisins and grapes, yeast bread dough, alcohol, raw eggs, fruit pits, nutmeg, and spoiled foods.

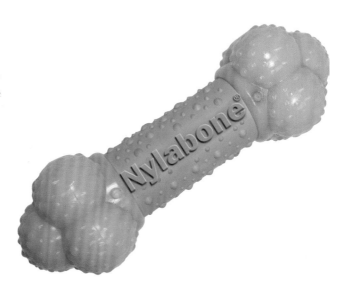

Chapter
5

Grooming Your Mastiff

If you think that only fluffy breeds need grooming, guess again. Every dog, regardless of size or coat length, deserves to have healthy skin, a clean, well-brushed coat, clipped nails, pain-free ears, and a mouthful of strong, sturdy teeth. After all, how would you feel if you never had a good soak or brushed your hair and teeth?

Your Mastiff is no exception. Regularly tidying up your dog has other benefits. Besides cutting down on shedding, you'll be able to spot any health issues and obtain veterinary treatment before they become major problems. Other pluses include having a pleasant-smelling Mastiff

around the house and setting aside a special time to focus on your dog's well-being. Turn a chore into a pamper session, and you'll discover a fun way to build a bond with your Mastiff.

Begin grooming your Mastiff a few days after bringing him home, but don't try to perform all of the spa jobs in one or two sessions—take things slowly. Simply let him sniff and investigate the tools. Progress to lightly brushing one part of his body, clipping one or two nails, or letting him lick the toothpaste off the brush.

If you have a puppy or an adult Mastiff who has never been groomed before, it will take time for him to become comfortable with the process. Try to remain patient if he fusses, and end the session early before he becomes too upset. Keep your grooming sessions positive by using treats and praise to reward your dog after you perform a grooming task.

To reduce cleanup, weather permitting, choose an outdoor area where you can groom your dog. If possible, ask someone to help you by holding the dog's collar to steady him, handing you grooming supplies, or just remaining with you for moral support.

Coat and Skin Care

Other than a little drool from time to time, one of the many nice things about Mastiffs is that they're basically a wash-and-wear dog. Their coats are fairly low

GROOMING AS A HEALTH CHECK

Sprucing up your Mastiff isn't about treating him to a day at the doggy spa. It's about providing preventive care, all in the comfort of your own home. Regularly bathing, brushing, cleaning your dog's ears, trimming his nails, and brushing his teeth doubles as a health checkup.

Grooming gives you the opportunity to feel that his skin is smooth, without lumps or bumps, and to make sure it is free of fleas or ticks. If you spot any minor cuts, you can clean them and apply antibacterial cream right away.

You'll also see that your dog's gums aren't red or swollen and that none of his teeth or nails are cracked or broken. Look at your dog's eyes and clean his ears and you'll know whether they're OK or showing signs of infection. And if you do spot a potential problem, the early detection allows you to obtain veterinary treatment before situations worsen. You can even save your dog's life.

maintenance, and they don't require expensive trips to a groomer. With the right tools and a little time and energy, you can easily keep your Mastiff's coat clean and fresh-smelling.

A glossy coat is a healthy coat. It shouldn't look dull and brittle, dry and flaky, or have bare spots with missing hair.

Brushing

Your Mastiff's coat isn't long, but it still needs some attention. A quick 5-minute light brushing once a day helps distribute the dog's natural oils throughout the coat and gives it a shine and natural luster. And, you'll pick up any debris and loose hair in the brush before it falls on your floors and furniture.

There's no need for heavy or harsh brushing with a bristle or wire-type brush, as the Mastiff's skin is sensitive and these brushes can easily scratch or damage the coat. The goal is not to strip out the healthy hair—just pick up the hair that's ready to come out on its own.

Some Mastiffs shed more hair than others, with the fawns carrying a slightly heavier undercoat, which sheds in a fluff. Brindle Mastiffs have less undercoat, but the main coat can often be slightly heavier and coarser and shed less. Shedding is a natural process, beginning with rapid growth in the spring, followed by slower growth, and ending in a resting stage. Mature hairs loosen in their follicles during winter. Shedding occurs when hair grows in the spring and pushes out the old, loose hairs.

How often this happens depends on several factors, including the dog, nutrition, the amount of sun or artificial light exposure, overall health, and stress. In cooler climates, Mastiffs grow thicker coats to help insulate them during the winter. Like many breeds, Mastiffs shed out their heavier coats during spring, when they no longer need extra protection. In the fall, they shed their thinner summer coats to begin adding a thicker coat to prepare for winter.

Brushing Supplies

- **Rubber grooming brush or rubber grooming glove**: a waterproof, dual-purpose tool. You can use it not only to brush him, but to help massage the shampoo into your dog's coat during bathing. This type of brush is designed to remove loose hair and collect it in the brush for easy removal.
- **Chamois cloth**: a wet chamois helps smooth down the coat after brushing and collects any loose hair.
- **Optional**: spray bottle filled with a solution of 1/2 a clear, antiseptic mouthwash and 1/2 water.

How to Brush Your Mastiff

At the first brushing session show your Mastiff the brush before proceeding. Let him sniff it so he feels comfortable with a strange object touching his body, then follow these easy steps:

1. Look over your dog and, using your open palm and fingers, feel his entire body, including his abdomen and groin area. This will let you know if he has any lumps or cuts that need attention. If you notice any odd bumps, make a note of the location or take a picture of that area and notify your veterinarian.

2. Brush in the direction the coat grows. Brushing against the direction can damage the coat and cause discomfort.

3. Brush both the top coat and the undercoat. Brushing only the top coat tangles up the undercoat, which is difficult to brush out.

4. Begin at the dog's head and don't forget the top of the head, cheeks, and around the ears. Continue down the neck, chest, and front legs.

5. In one long stroke, brush from the head toward the tail, down the hips, rear legs—both front and back—and along the sides of your dog's body. Continue down the front legs, chest, and abdomen.

6. If the brush fills with hair along the way, remove it, dispose of it in a wastebasket, and continue brushing. Depending on how much your dog is shedding, you may have to clean the brush a few times.

7. Until your dog is accustomed to the process, he may fuss. If so, don't

GROOMING CHECKLIST

✓ Brush the coat daily.
✓ Bathe once a month.
✓ Check the eyes and ears daily.

✓ Trim the nails weekly.
✓ Brush the teeth daily.

worry about brushing his whole body all at once, especially since a Mastiff is a lot of dog to brush. Divide the task into a few sessions and when you are finished, reward your dog with a treat or a toy so he associates grooming with a reward for good behavior.

8. Wet the chamois cloth and rub it over your dog's body. This picks up all the loose hairs the brush might have missed. It also adds polish to the coat.

9. You can also spritz his body with the mouthwash-water mixture. This gives the coat a fresh smell and a nice shine. The antiseptic mouthwash contains soothing herbal oils (thymol, eucalyptol, menthol, methyl salicylate) that often help repel gnats and mosquitoes as well.

Bathing

A healthy Mastiff coat is a clean coat, and regular bathing keeps the skin free of debris and odor. Contrary to popular opinion, bathing does not dry out the coat. Mastiffs who are exhibited in the show ring are bathed before every show, which may be every week or every other week, and their coats are smooth and shiny.

If you're not showing your Mastiff, how often you bathe him depends on how much natural oil his coat secretes, which produces a greasy look and feel, and how much time he spends exercising outdoors. For the active dog who hikes or participates in other canine sports a few times a week, a bath once every three to four weeks may be sufficient. For the Mastiff who spends most of his time indoors, a good washing about once every six weeks works well.

Brush your dog before giving him a bath. If he has any mats and they become wet during bathing, moisture can be trapped close to the skin and cause infection. Brushing before bathing also avoids excess hair clogging the drain.

Bathing Supplies

• **Canine shampoo:** choose a shampoo formulated for dogs, as the pH in human shampoo is too high for dogs and often too harsh on the coat. Oatmeal or

If the weather is warm, towel your dog off and let him drip dry outdoors.

hypoallergenic shampoos help soothe skin problems.

- **Water bucket or a hand-held shower sprayer:** use to easily wet your dog and thoroughly rinse out the shampoo.
- **Small towel or cotton balls:** use to dry the inside portion of your dog's ears after bathing.
- **Large towels or pet hair dryer:** human hair dryers are too hot for a dog's skin and coat.
- **Non-slip rubber mats:** gives your dog some traction in the shower stall.

How to Bathe Your Mastiff

Washing a Mastiff off can be as simple as sponging him off outdoors with some soap and a bucket of warm water, or made more complex with a walk-in visit to your shower. Whichever way works for you, make sure it's easy enough that you'll do it whenever your dog needs a good cleaning.

Give your dog the cue to stay or ask someone to assist you by holding your dog's collar to prevent him from walking away while he's still wet. While bathing, keep the area draft-free and follow these steps:

1. Place one or two nonslip mats beneath your dog's feet to prevent him from slipping.
2. Using warm (not hot!) water, spray your dog's feet before dampening the rest of his body, being careful not to get water inside his ears or eyes.
3. To clean around your dog's face, wipe the area with a damp cloth.
4. Dab a small circle of shampoo on the top of his head, along his back, and down his sides. Don't get soap in his eyes!
5. Using the rubber brush and a circular motion, massage the shampoo into his coat.
6. Thoroughly rinse the shampoo out of the coat. Use the brush while rinsing to remove any residual shampoo. Leftover shampoo can irritate his skin

BATHING A MASTIFF

Q: Is it hard to bathe a Mastiff?

A: You don't need to take your Mastiff to a professional groomer to maintain his coat in good condition. If you have a bucket of water, one or two bath sheets, a wash cloth, and a rubber brush, you can easily do the job yourself. You can forget about having to get him in and out of the bathtub, too, because you don't want him to fall and injure himself. Put one or two non-skid bath mats on the floor of your stall shower and carefully walk him into the shower. Once he becomes accustomed to the routine, the job goes quickly.

—Dr. William R. Newman, longtime Mastiff owner, Vice-President of the Mastiff Club of America, and vice chairman of the American Kennel Club (AKC) Board of Directors

and dull his coat. If you're unsure whether all the soap is out, rinse again.

7. If the weather is warm, towel your dog off and let him drip dry outdoors. During cooler weather, dry him thoroughly with towels and follow up with a pet hair dryer. Set the dryer on a low or cool setting to avoid damage to the coat, frequently move the dryer nozzle, and keep the dryer at least 6 inches (15 cm) away your dog's body.

8. Using a small towel or cotton balls, thoroughly dry the inside folds of your Mastiff's ears.

9. Dry your Mastiff's neck and throat areas thoroughly before putting his collar back on. Trapping wet hair beneath the collar creates the perfect medium for bacteria growth.

Hopefully, he'll resist the urge to roll in the yard and dirty himself up all over again!

Dental Care

Taking care of your Mastiff's teeth begins the day after you bring him home and continues for his lifetime. To avoid canine dental disease, teach him early on to allow you to brush his teeth. Daily brushing, applying an oral dental spray or gel, and a yearly professional cleaning help remove food particles, bacteria, or the plaque that forms and causes periodontal disease.

According to the American Veterinary Medical Association (AVMA), 80 percent of dogs show signs of oral disease by age three. The signs of oral disease include bad breath, brown color on the teeth, cracked or worn teeth, changes in appetite, excessive drooling or pawing at the mouth, and bleeding gums. When ignored, dental disease leads to infections that can spread to internal organs.

Dental Care Supplies

- **Canine oral hygiene spray or gel**: this loosens plaque and tartar and helps reverse oral disease. When applied, it mixes with your dog's saliva to coat the teeth and kill harmful bacteria. Use daily after brushing.
- **Canine toothbrush**: choose the large-breed size. This pet dental toothbrush has gentle nylon bristles on three sides that clean each tooth on the top, front, and back. The ergonomic handle makes it easier to use than a toothbrush made for people.
- **Canine toothpaste**: helps control plaque, fights bad breath, and comes in a variety of flavors. It's specially formulated for dogs and doesn't require

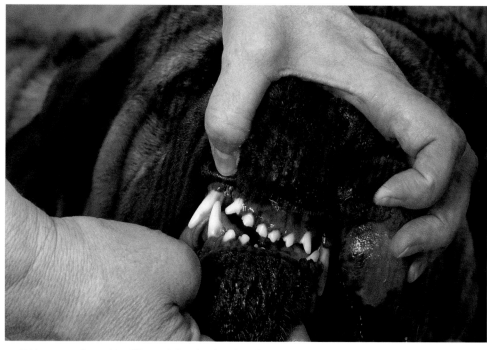

Taking care of your Mastiff's teeth begins the day after you bring him home and continues for his lifetime.

rinsing. Do not use toothpaste made for people, as it can cause stomach upset in dogs.

How to Brush Your Dog's Teeth

Once you and your Mastiff become comfortable with the process, brushing your dog's teeth takes minutes once a day. For the first few sessions, put some canine toothpaste on your fingers and let him lick it off. Formulated to dissolve in your dog's mouth, your dog will like the taste. Graduate to adding some paste to the canine toothbrush and let him lick it off the brush.

To progress to brushing all of the teeth, follow these easy steps:

1. Place one hand beneath your dog's chin and use your other hand to show him the brush with the paste.
2. When he begins to lick the paste off, slowly insert the brush into his mouth.
3. For the first few sessions, brush one or two teeth you can easily reach; at subsequent sessions, lift your dog's lips to brush additional teeth.
4. Brush the tooth in a circular motion, with the brush at a 45-degree angle to the gum line. Brush the front and side teeth. To reach the top and bottom molars in the back, lift your dog's lips.
5. Once or twice a day, apply oral hygiene spray or gel to your dog's teeth.

Once a year, your veterinarian should look at your dog's teeth during the yearly examination. She may or may not recommend a professional cleaning to take care of those hard-to-reach areas of your dog's mouth.

Ear Care

In proportion to a Mastiff's skull, the V-shaped ears are relatively small, but they still need regular cleaning to remain healthy. Your Mastiff's hanging ears trap moisture and debris in the ear canal, which makes it an ideal site for bacterial or yeast infections, and ear mites.

To prevent ear infections, keep the ears dry and clean. When healthy, the ear should have a pleasant odor. When infected, the ear has a musky, foul smell. Scratching or rubbing his ears on the ground, shaking his head, or tilting his ear to one side are all signs of infection.

Check your dog's ears once a day. If you detect a foul smell, they need cleaning.

Ear Cleaning Supplies

- **Medicated ear cleaning solution with a low alcohol content, sterile mineral oil, or almond oil**: loosens and dissolves earwax. Ask your veterinarian to recommend a cleaner, or use mineral or almond oil.
- **Cotton strips**: use long strips of cotton to remove ear debris. Don't insert cotton applicators, cotton balls, or makeup remover pads into the ear, as these

may injure the ear and can't reach the earwax lodged deeply inside the ear.

How to Clean Your Mastiff's Ears

To remove debris and clean your dog's ears, follow these steps:

1. Lift the ear flap.
2. Insert a few drops of ear cleaner into the ear opening.
3. Gently massage the base of the ear a few seconds to loosen the debris. You should hear a squishing sound.
4. Don't worry if your dog shakes his head and ejects the solution and debris.
5. Gently insert a cotton strip into the ear opening and wipe out the inside of the ear.

Don't insert cotton applicator swabs or anything pointed or sharp into the canal, as this pushes the debris into the canal rather than extracting it.

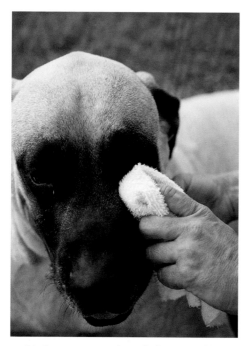

Gently remove any clear discharge or dried mucus with a cloth moistened with warm water.

Eye Care

Check the corner of your dog's eyes daily for the presence of any discharge or dried mucus that may accumulate. Gently remove any clear discharge or dried mucus by moistening a cotton ball or cloth with warm water and wiping the debris from the inside corner of the eye outward.

A watery discharge from one eye or a yellow-green or pus-like eye discharge from one or both eyes may signal a serious infection requiring veterinary attention.

Facial Care

Pay special attention to the lips and skin folds around your dog's mouth and keep them clean. Perpetually wet, this moisture can allow skin bacteria to build up and cause an infection on the lips. Sometimes there's a foul odor, too. To alleviate the problem, use veterinary medicated wipes or dampen a washcloth, wipe the area clean, and dry it thoroughly once a day. If

Introduce nail trimming the day after you bring your dog home and do it gradually.

you notice lesions or pimples around this area, take your dog to the veterinarian. A topical medication or a medicated bath may provide soothing relief.

Nail Care

Mastiffs have thick, strong nails and keeping them short can be a challenge, but it's all part of good grooming. It's a myth that dogs who spend much of their time walking on concrete will naturally wear down their nails. Like people, dogs' nails grow at different rates, depending on body chemistry, nutrition, and the shape of the nails. Some dogs' nails grow like weeds and need a good trim every week no matter where they exercise, while other dogs' nails remain short for longer stretches.

A dog's nails should not touch the ground, thus allowing the dog to stand firmly on the pads of his feet. When nails are too long, they force the dog's weight onto the back of the foot and cause foot injuries. Another hazard, nails that are too long are easily broken, torn, or snagged.

GROOMING YOUR PUPPY

Bathing, brushing, and giving your puppy a pedicure helps keep him in good condition, but it's also a great opportunity to begin building a trusting relationship. By creating a grooming ritual, your Mastiff will know what to expect from you, and he can relax during the experience.

To make him feel more comfortable with the feel of your hands on his body during grooming, pet your puppy from head to toe at least once a day. When you progress to brushing or bathing, he may wiggle because he doesn't understand why you want him to stand still. That's OK. Give him the cue to *stay*, and give him a small food treat when he remains in one place for a few minutes.

When should you begin grooming your puppy? Start a few days after bringing him home. Brush his coat and one or two of his teeth, plus give his nails a quick trim, although he may not need a bath for two or three weeks.

By scheduling frequent, short sessions and always ending with something he likes, such as a treat or a game with a special toy, he won't dread the tidying-up process. If you begin to feel frustrated, end the session so he doesn't pick up on your negative emotion. Soon he'll look forward to the hands-on time he has with you and won't object to being touched.

Introduce nail trimming the day after you bring your dog home and do it gradually. It helps to have good tools and an abundance of patience. Some Mastiff owners use clippers to take off the tips of the nails, then follow-up with an electric nail grinder with variable speeds and a sanding attachment to get a close trim.

A blood vessel, called the "quick," runs through the middle of the nail. If you nick the quick, it will bleed. However, don't let your fear of trimming a nail too short and causing it to bleed prevent you from getting the job done. Even experienced groomers clip a nail too close occasionally. If you accidently cut the quick, hold a wet washcloth to the tip for a few minutes to stop the bleeding. For bigger bleeds, use cornstarch or styptic powder.

Once your dog accepts having his feet handled and you learn to clip his nails, the job will get easier.

Nail Trimming Supplies

- **Canine nail clippers**: choose the largest size nail trimmer type that you're comfortable using, such as the guillotine or scissor-action style.

- **Cornstarch or styptic powder or pencil**: stops the bleeding if you nick the sensitive center of the nail, or the "quick," during nail trimming.
- **Electric nail grinder**: choose a corded or cordless model and use the sanding head. Grinders have varying speeds so you can slowly trim the nail without taking off too much of the nail too quickly.
- **Small food treats**: use to reward your dog when he stands politely and allows you to clip a few nails.

How to Trim the Nails

For best results, clip your dog's nails once a week by following these easy steps:

1. Place your Mastiff in a sitting position or let him lie on the floor. Allow him to sniff the clippers and/or grinder before turning it on. If your dog is startled by the noise of the grinder, give him a small food treat and turn the grinder off and on several times until it no longer bothers him. Soon he'll begin to associate receiving a reward with the noise. This may take several sessions.

2. With your dog facing you, lift one foot. Clip or grind off the little hook at the end of one of the nails that extends past the quick. On black nails this may be difficult to locate, so look underneath the nail to find where the tip curves slightly downward.

3. Clip or grind another nail. If your dog isn't cooperative, put the foot back down before trying another nail. Hold the paw firmly but not so tightly that he fights you. Give your dog a treat when he lets you hold his foot and clip one nail.

4. Add nails as your dog allows, but don't give up.

Remember that you're doing this for his health so it's important to clip his nails regularly. With practice, you will improve your nail-trimming skills.

Chapter
6

Training Your Mastiff

Welcoming a new Mastiff puppy or adult into your family definitely calls for a celebration. It's an exciting time, and this jumbo-size canine will change your life and household forever. But, when your dog looks up at you with soft eyes of adoration, he may actually be thinking about how he's going to maneuver you into doing his bidding. He's a sensitive but clever creature, and in no time he'll coax you into submission—if you let him.

Here's where implementing some positive training methods, along with having some patience and a good sense of humor, will help you teach your dog some basic house rules. Start by socializing your Mastiff to his new community, introducing a crate, and showing him appropriate places to potty outdoors.

Puppies and adult dogs will benefit from learning these new skills. When bringing a rescue Mastiff into your home, assume that he has never learned household manners. Begin training him as if he were a puppy and has everything to learn.

Why Train Your Mastiff?

Living with a 200-pound (91-kg) dog means uttering the phrase "whoa, boy" on more than one occasion. While a single word or two is often enough to direct your Mastiff to make the right choice, this is, after all, a breed with girth. Without realizing it, he can send a toddler flying with a slight bump or clear a coffee table of snacks and glassware in a single bound.

Knowing how to behave in and out of the house and around people doesn't come naturally to any dog. Like other dogs, Mastiffs need to learn these lessons. Fortunately, they catch on quickly and are capable of following your directions once they understand your expectations.

Your Mastiff will benefit from training. While you may not care whether your dog sits and heels perfectly on cue, the better he performs these behaviors, the better he will behave in the house. He needs to learn the basics: to sit, lie down and chill out when you ask him to, come when called, walk politely on a leash, and greet people without knocking them over. You also want your Mastiff to learn not to guard his toys or food, and to accept attention from admirers.

Don't worry that training your Mastiff is cruel and inhumane treatment, or that it will rob him of his personality or transform him into some giant robot. If you use modern, positive methods with rewards for compliance instead of physical force, your Mastiff will thrive and look forward to his lessons. Through practice sessions, he learns how to listen closely, how to understand what you say to him, and how to comply with your directions. In the process, you and your

TRAINING CHECKLIST

✓ Train with positive methods using praise, treats, toys, or a game.

✓ Begin socializing your Mastiff to children and other dogs right away.

✓ Introduce the crate on day one.

✓ Housetraining starts the day your Mastiff comes home.

✓ Teach basic cues of *sit, come, stay, down,* and *walk nicely on a leash.*

dog will develop a sweet bond that will last a lifetime.

Positive Training

Positive training focuses on showing your dog what you want him to do and rewarding him with praise, affection, food treats, toys, or a game when he does it. When reinforced for complying, the dog will repeat the behavior to earn the reward again. This method does not use force, fear, or intimidation. Who wouldn't want a reward for good behavior instead of punishment for bad?

Animal behaviorists believe that the old methods of harsh corrections that included rolling a dog on his back (which is pretty hard to do with a Mastiff anyway), yanking or shocking with a special collar, throwing choke chains, or pinching are ineffective. These may get a dog's attention the first time, but in the long run these abusive methods will make the dog fearful of the trainer and everyone else around him. When pushed

like this, many Mastiffs will simply shut down and refuse to do anything you want.

The question always comes up about what to do if your dog makes a mistake during training. Do you give him a treat anyway? No. Only reward your dog when he does what you want and ignore the negative. If your dog continually jumps up on you, for example, pretend he isn't there. He wants your attention—when you yell, push, or pet him, he'll continue to jump because he's receiving the attention he wants. When you ignore him, he realizes that when he jumps he receives nothing from you, which should stop the unwanted behavior.

Socialization

When you acquire a Mastiff puppy or adult, you also become his social director. He's ready to make a grand entrance into the world, and he needs you to introduce him to people, dogs, places, and experiences in a safe, non-threatening way. Socialization teaches your dog how to understand his

Your Mastiff is sensitive, so using positive methods is the best way to train him.

environment and those around him.

The process begins the day you bring him home and continues well into adulthood. Puppies between 8 and 16 weeks of age will soak up every new experience, develop lasting impressions, and take things in stride. This small window of opportunity in a Mastiff's life is critical to his social development and will impact his behavior as an adult. When older puppies have not been well socialized during this important period of time, they have a tendency to grow up nervous, shy, and fearful. They find it difficult to cope with odd noises, such as thunder or cars backfiring, and changes in their environment.

The American Veterinary Society of Animal Behavior (AVSAB) believes that puppies should be exposed to as many new people, animals, stimuli, and environments as possible within the first three months of life. This should be accomplished without overstimulating puppies and causing excessive fear, withdrawal, or avoidance behavior, and before puppies are fully vaccinated. However, until your puppy is fully vaccinated, it's wise to avoid being around potentially unvaccinated dogs. Take your dog for a car ride, visit stores that allow dogs, or make dates with friends with dogs. Skip places where stray dogs may visit, such as the dog park or dog-friendly beaches.

How to Socialize Your Mastiff Puppy

According to canine behaviorists, you should socialize your dog by the "Rule of Sevens." This means that by seven weeks of age a puppy should have walked on seven different surfaces, played with seven different objects, visited seven different locations, met seven new people, been exposed to seven challenges, eaten from seven different containers, and eaten in seven different locations. A good breeder will likely accomplish this goal before the puppy goes to his new home.

By all means, continue this practice after you bring your Mastiff home by gradually exposing him to a variety of situations. You don't need to spend hours socializing your Mastiff puppy because it's the quality, not the quantity, that counts. Setting aside 10 to 20 minutes several times a week pays big dividends—as long as you don't overwhelm your puppy. As your Mastiff grows, you can add more time. Slowly introduce him to new people and places, as these new experiences reassure your dog that nothing will hurt him. Your goal is to make your puppy comfortable in safe surroundings. In the beginning, avoid crowds, as too much commotion is overwhelming. Skip odd people, dogs, or situations. If you feel uncomfortable, chances are your puppy will feel the same way, so avoid these types of encounters.

Walk him through different neighborhoods, go inside buildings, and stroll through outdoor shopping malls, garden centers, and car washes. Don't let noisy car horns, garbage trucks, construction sites, and sirens dissuade you from getting your dog out and about. These help build your dog's confidence and strengthen his curiosity about the world. Let your Mastiff puppy explore different surfaces, such as gravel, sand, tile, and grass, and take him around moving objects, including children on skateboards, shopping carts, wheelchairs,

and strollers. A puppy who is never exposed to things with wheels may be fearful of them and try to go after them as he matures.

If your puppy seems fearful, resist the urge to coddle or reassure him that everything is OK. This only reinforces his fear. It's best to ignore his hesitation and scale back the exposure to quieter experiences. When your Mastiff appears confident and curious, praise him with a small food treat and tell him he's a "Good dog!"

Get your puppy used to all kinds of surroundings.

To help with socialization, give some serious thought to signing your puppy up for puppy kindergarten classes. Open to dogs between the ages of 12 weeks and 6 months, these classes provide your puppy with a variety of experiences in a safe, structured setting. Choose a class that offers positive, reward-based training through play, toys, and treats. Continue the socialization process until your puppy reaches adulthood, as one puppy kindergarten or basic training class at six months of age isn't enough. That's because some dogs who may be well socialized early in life can become shy, fearful, and/or aggressive later on—usually around eight months to two years of age. This new behavior can be triggered by a number of reasons, such as a change in family situations or a lack of new experiences. Why some dogs feel these effects more so than others is uncertain.

To continue socialization into adulthood, spend a few minutes taking your Mastiff along with you on errands, walking a new route, or visiting friends with dogs. New sights and sounds work wonders to maintain your dog's comfort level.

As working dogs, well-socialized Mastiffs usually get along well with other dogs.

Even if your dog seems well-adjusted at home, don't think your job is done. Keep socializing him to avoid boredom, territorial barking, and other problems later on.

Socializing Adult Dogs

If you adopt an older dog, don't believe the saying "you can't teach an old dog new tricks" because it's simply not true. Many senior canines can overcome emotional baggage with good socialization. The goal is to teach your adult dog appropriate behavior.

Begin slowly with treats to enhance all new experiences. Invite one or two friends over who are comfortable around a giant breed, and ask them to feed your dog a few goodies. If finding dog-savvy people is difficult, enroll your dog in a positive-training obedience class.

To introduce other dogs, don't take your Mastiff to a dog park. Most adult dogs do not enjoy playing with large groups of unfamiliar dogs. He needs to visit areas where he can see other dogs without being forced to interact. Give your dog a treat when another dog comes into view. If your dog barks and refuses the treat, move further away. In future encounters move closer to the other dog, and reward your dog when he doesn't bark. Or, get your dog's attention and walk away from the other dog.

How to Socialize Your Mastiff to Other Pets

If your new Mastiff will be joining another dog at home, introduce them on a leash, outside the home, on neutral territory. This gives both dogs time to get to know one another. After they've spent some time together outside, take the new puppy into the house first. Let him spend plenty of time looking around and feeling comfortable before bringing in the resident dog. Keep both leashes on so you can grab them in an emergency, and let them trail the leashes until you feel comfortable. Give both dogs plenty of room, and try to remain calm. If you feel apprehensive, your dogs will pick up on that emotion. For the first few days, separate the dogs when you have to leave them unattended.

As working dogs, Mastiffs get along with other dogs, but there are some restrictions. Mastiffs, like most breeds, have a strong prey drive. This means they will likely bolt after, pounce on, and grab small animals. This includes cats and small dogs. In the process of pursuit, the dog could injure himself by running into traffic or cause harm and even sudden death to the other animal.

How to Socialize Your Mastiff to Children

Kids and Mastiffs can go together like peanut butter and jelly, but you have

TRAINING WITH OTHER DOGS AROUND

If you have multiple dogs in the household, it's often a challenge to train a puppy. Everyone vies for your attention and puts on a show for a treat. When training your puppy, go it alone. Take your puppy to another room and close the door. Or, put the other dogs in their crates or in a separate location. In this way, you can give your puppy personal attention without him having to compete with the other dogs.

to teach both how to interact with one another safely. Begin the minute you bring your new puppy home. Establish some guidelines (see Chapter 2 for more information) and explain to your child how to act around the puppy. Always supervise all interactions between them, even with the most laid-back Mastiff. While it's a good idea to let your child participate in your puppy's care, never force or expect your child to be solely responsible. Caring for a dog is a family project.

Crate Training

A Mastiff crate may loom large in your home, but when used properly, it's a wonderfully safe place for a dog to hang out. Invaluable during housetraining, it ensures that your puppy will not potty where he sleeps. For those times when you can't keep an eye on your puppy or he needs to stay out of the way during repair projects for a few hours, a crate comes in handy.

The act of putting your dog into his crate and taking him out also helps establish your leadership during training. Never think of your dog's crate as a jail, or a place of confinement for long hours during the day. Your Mastiff needs to spend the majority of his time with you and not in his crate. If your breeder did not crate-train your Mastiff, it will take some time for your pup to learn how to use it, but with minimal training, he'll soon regard it as a cozy retreat.

How to Crate Train

To introduce a crate to your Mastiff, associate it with positive rewards, such as meals, treats, toys, security, and sleep. Never put anything inside the crate, such as a blanket, rug, towels, or a dog mat that your dog can chew up and that may cause a choking incident when he's left unsupervised.

Open the crate door and place a food treat inside. Encourage your puppy to enter and explore. When he goes inside, praise him by saying, "Good boy!" Lure your Mastiff inside the crate with his food bowl. If he's comfortable, close the door for a minute. Don't leave your dog alone. Open the door and praise him. Repeat again with a treat, and close the door. Gradually increase the time he spends inside, up to an hour during the day.

If you know that your puppy does not have to potty and he whines or cries, resist the urge to let him out or try to soothe him. This only reinforces his reluctance to stay inside. Wait for him to be quiet before letting him out. Always give your puppy a treat when he goes into the crate.

If you must leave the house for more than an hour or two at a time, consider using an exercise pen for your puppy instead of a crate. This gives him more room to play and move around, but still keeps him confined to one area.

Housetraining

When your Mastiff lived at the breeder's,

When housetraining, choose a spot outside that your dog can easily get to.

he knew where to potty, but at your home he doesn't have a clue. Everything seems unfamiliar to him, especially with new textures to walk on. It's no surprise that your puppy will potty where he feels comfortable. If your puppy was raised in an outdoor kennel, it may take longer to housetrain him, as he may not recognize that your backyard is the bathroom locale. But with time and patience, he'll soon find his own sweet spot.

How to Housetrain

Begin training your Mastiff the first or second day you bring him home. Establish a schedule for when he will need to potty:

- immediately in the morning when he wakes up
- about 15 minutes after drinking water
- about 30 minutes after eating
- immediately after waking from a nap
- about once an hour during playtime during the day
- right before bedtime

If you are totally committed to keeping a regular schedule, your Mastiff will quickly learn where and when to potty in the appropriate location. If you can't watch your puppy for signs that he needs to go outside, place him in his crate. Puppies will not potty where they sleep.

Choose a spot outside that your dog can easily get to. Mastiffs are intelligent and want to have their own place. Adhering to the schedule of when your Mastiff needs to potty, take him out on a leash and remain standing in the designated area. The leash prevents him from getting too distracted with such a variety of sights, smells, and sounds. He'll sniff around and when he's finished, he'll do his business. Praise him lavishly in an upbeat, happy tone of voice when he eliminates.

Resist the urge to walk to another location if he doesn't potty right away. If you do, he'll continue to be stimulated by new smells, which only prolongs his search for the right location. By keeping him on the leash, he'll return to the same spot every time, which makes clean up so much easier. After a while, you can take the leash off.

Choose a phrase to say every time you take him outside, such as "hurry, hurry," or "get busy," and he'll soon associate urinating and defecating with hearing those words.

If he makes a mistake in the house, just clean it up promptly with an enzymatic cleaner. This destroys the odor-causing molecules in the eliminations and discourages your dog from returning to the same spot. Don't punish your puppy because he won't understand a connection between the puddle and a reprimand. If you catch him in the act, pick him up if you can, or immediately guide him outdoors to the potty area. Praise him if he finishes there.

TRAINING A MASTIFF

Q: What is the best way to train a Mastiff?

A: Most Mastiffs are highly food-motivated, so use a food lure and lots of praise to teach the basics of *sit, stay,* and *down.* Hold the food just above your dog's head, and he'll move automatically into a sit. When you put the food near the ground and in between the dog's front legs, he'll naturally move down. Say a specific word of command with each of these in a quiet environment, and he'll learn the basics in no time.

Once your dog has learned the basics, use the food sporadically as a reward rather than as a lure. This is the key to training. Add distractions or different environments. If you don't get a response after asking your Mastiff to perform a command, don't keep repeating it. Mastiffs are great at ignoring requests and commands if they are asked multiple times and there's no compliance.

If your dog doesn't comply on the first command, help him to complete the task. Once he understands what it is you want, repeat the cue. Mastiffs are very smart and, as a working breed, will make their own decisions if they become confused.

To teach your Mastiff to perform little tricks, watch what your dog does. If you see a behavior you like that he does naturally, such as rolling on his back, put a word to it and reward him every time he does it.

—Nicki Camerra, Mastiff owner and trainer of the most
American Kennel Club (AKC) Utility-titled Mastiffs

Basic Obedience Commands

Whether you want to become a serious obedience competitor or just want your Mastiff to mind his p's and q's at home and in public, you should teach him a minimum of five basic behaviors: *sit, come, stay, down,* and walk nicely on a leash. By the time your puppy is four to six months old, he should know these five commands.

When training your Mastiff remember the following:

• Introduce a new behavior in a familiar environment that has few distractions, such as your yard or house.
• Keep training fun.
• Use your dog's name first, followed by the cue. (When you want him to stay, it's not necessary to use his name first.)
• Use verbal praise and food treats to

reward your dog. Offer soft goodies, such as small cubes of cheese or pieces of hot dogs, rather than biscuit-like hard treats. Soft treats take less time for your dog to chew so he'll quickly want to repeat the desired behavior.

• Be consistent when giving cues.
• Keep lessons short.
• Don't repeat cues.

When taking your Mastiff outdoors for training around distractions, keep the tastier treats inside your pocket or in a fanny pack. For indoor training, you can use kibble or biscuits. Place the treats in tightly covered containers, up high in different rooms of the house. This enables you to instantly reward your dog for listening to your cues. If you notice that your dog isn't paying as close attention as he did when you began your training, change the treat to a really tasty tidbit he's never had before.

Sit

The easiest behavior for puppies and adult dogs to learn, the *sit* is the go-to command when you need to establish some control. Asking your dog to sit reinforces his position as a family member who must abide by the rules you set. Use it if your Mastiff becomes overly exuberant, before his meals, when guests come to visit, and prior to going in and out of the house.

The *sit* is the go-to command when you need to establish some control.

How to Teach Sit

1. Begin with your dog on leash; this helps if he is easily distracted.
2. With the leash in one hand and a treat in the other hand, show your dog the tidbit by holding it close to and slightly above his nose.
3. When he lifts his nose to sniff the food, say, "Sit."
4. Slowly move the treat over his head, toward the back of his body. If he jumps up or lifts his front off the ground, you're probably holding the

food too high. When a dog walks backward, you're likely holding the treat too low or too far back.

5. When he drops into a sitting position, reward him with the tidbit and praise him with "Good sit" in an upbeat tone of voice.

6. Let him know that it's OK to stand up again with a release word, such as "OK," and pet him for a few seconds.

Repeat the *sit* exercise several times, a few times a day.

Come

Training your Mastiff to come to you reliably and immediately when you call him may save his life. While some Mastiffs never want to venture too far out of your sight, others are inquisitive and think nothing of wandering off to check out an interesting person, dog, or smell. In the process, they can run into traffic or toward other danger.

When you say "Come!" to your dog, he needs to understand that you mean right now. Never use it to reprimand your dog or to end something fun he's involved in, such as playtime. Otherwise, he learns to ignore you. Always acknowledge his willingness to come to you with praise, affection, treats, or all three.

How to Teach Come

1. Start by filling your pocket with treats and standing in front of your dog.

Say his name and give him a treat. Wait five minutes and repeat. Repeat several times, but wait until he isn't paying attention to you. Say his name. If he turns to look at you, say "Yes!" and give him a treat. Repeat.

2. Inside the house, call his name, add "Come," and run away from him in the opposite direction.

3. When he comes to you, praise him and give him a tidbit. Repeat. Once he reliably responds, move the practice session outdoors to a fenced area or clip his leash onto his collar.

4. Call his name, followed by "Come!" Move away from him. Praise and treat.

5. Practice around other distractions.

Down

Another practical command, the *down* is useful when you want your dog to lie down and relax while you are occupied. A *down* comes in handy if your dog has to wait at the veterinarian's office, if your friends come to visit, or if he needs to cool off underneath a shady tree during outdoor exercise. This submissive position for a dog may be more challenging to teach a Mastiff, but with patience, practice, and persistence, your dog can do it.

How to Teach Down

1. Begin with your puppy sitting in front of you.

2. Hold a treat in front of his nose. Gradually move the tidbit down in front of your dog's paws, toward the ground, while you say, "Down!" It's important to move the treat down and then forward—otherwise your pup will stand and walk toward the treat.
3. When he lowers his body all the way down, praise and give him the treat.
4. Repeat several times.

Stay

The *stay* command is an important one that your dog should follow. When you tell your dog to "stay," it means don't move, no matter what position he's in—usually a *sit* or a *down*—until you give him a release to move. If the door suddenly opens and your Mastiff is tempted to run after another dog, the *stay* command may help keep him at your side.

How to Teach Stay

1. Start with your Mastiff in a *sit* or a *down* position.
2. Stand in front of him and say, "Stay," while using a stop signal of holding your open palm in front of his nose.

Walking a Mastiff without him pulling on the leash is a must.

3. Immediately say, "Good!" and give him a treat. If your dog doesn't move, repeat "Good!" and give him another treat.

4. Wait a moment, then say, "OK" and move away from him. Hopefully, he will stand and move around. If he remains in the stay position, repeat "OK" and give him a big pat on the chest so he gets the idea to move.

5. Repeat several times, moving to different locations in your home. Gradually give the command and move farther away from him. Add distractions to the exercise.

Walk Nicely on a Leash

Walking a Mastiff without him pulling on the leash is a must. You simply can't have a 150-pound (68-kg) dog yanking you down the street. If you start training your puppy while he's small and around three months of age, it will be much easier than waiting until he's full-grown. Adult Mastiffs can be taught to walk on a leash, too. It just takes a little more strength and patience on your part. Use a buckle collar—never a choke-chain—on your dog, and carry some treats in your pocket.

How to Teach Walk Nicely on a Leash

1. Hold the leash in your right hand and ask your dog to sit on your left side. Position your left hand halfway down the leash.

2. Say, "Let's Go!" and walk forward.

3. After a few steps with your dog on your left side, praise him and give him a tidbit. The idea is to reward him when he walks politely by your side without pulling.

4. If your puppy is jumping or walking into you to get to the food, hold the food lower but only give it to him when he doesn't jump.

5. If your puppy pulls ahead, simply stop. Don't jerk the leash or yell at him. He'll soon figure out that when he walks nicely, he gets to go forward. When he pulls, you stop.

Walking your dog should be a pleasant, relaxing experience. If it isn't, take the time to properly train your dog to behave on walks. The effort is worth it.

FINDING A TRAINER

Congratulations! You've decided to find a dog trainer for you and your Mastiff. A class instructor can help start your puppy off on the right paw, or perhaps your Mastiff joined your family as an adult and you don't know what his puppyhood was like or what sort of temperament his parents had.

To begin your search:

- Ask your veterinarian, breeder, or other dog-owning friends for referrals. People like to recommend a good professional and seldom hesitate to tell stories about the problem ones.

- Contact professional dog training organizations that list trainers in your area, such as the Association of Pet Dog Trainers (www.apdt.com), the National Association of Dog Obedience Instructors (www.nadoi.org), or the International Association of Animal Behavior Consultants (www.iaabc.org).

- Check the American Kennel Club (AKC) website (www.akc.org) under the "Training Clubs" section for a list of training clubs in your area.

Once you've narrowed down a few trainers, contact them to learn more specific information:

- Inquire about training philosophy and how the trainer handles problem behaviors.

- Find out about background, experience, certification, and references.

- Ask the trainer if she has experience with a giant breed and would feel comfortable if your Mastiff joined the class.

- Ask if you can visit a class before signing up so you can observe trainers' methods and how owners and their dogs react.

During your visits:

- Pay close attention to how the trainer treats the dogs. Does she praise and reward dogs for appropriate behavior, or use harsh corrections?

- Observe whether the owners and dogs are enjoying their learning experience.

- Is the class well-organized? Does the trainer give clear instructions the owners can follow easily?

- Is there enough space in the class area to comfortably accommodate eight to ten puppies per class? Are the facilities well-lit and safe?

- Is there an assistant to help owners if the instructor works with another owner?

Once you select a class and begin attending, don't feel shy about asking the trainer to repeat instructions. It's easy to feel overwhelmed with the new knowledge you're acquiring. If you ever feel uncomfortable with another dog or owner in the class, the instructor's methods or personality, or the facilities, don't hesitate to opt out of future sessions and choose another trainer.

Chapter
7

Solving Problems
With Your Mastiff

Understanding everything that your Mastiff is thinking is one of life's little mysteries. Although dogs are good at reading human body language, people have much to learn about what goes on inside those wonderful canine heads. Since no dog is always an angel, count on your Mastiff to do some things he shouldn't. You can probably forgive some everyday Mastiff mischief, but if he causes a serious problem that's difficult to live with, it's time to do something.

Problem Behaviors

Just because your Mastiff is a big, powerful dog doesn't mean that you must solve an offensive behavior with force.

Anger and violence are never appropriate and will do more harm than good.

A 2009 study by the University of Pennsylvania published in *Applied Animal Behavior Science* (Elsevier) showed that aggressive dogs trained with aggressive, confrontational, or aversive training techniques, such as hitting, staring, growling, or rolling them onto their backs, continued their aggressive ways. Non-aversive training methods, such as exercise or rewards, were more successful in reducing or eliminating aggressive responses.

Your Mastiff wants to please you. However, when he displays disruptive behavior, such as barking, chewing or digging, urinating in the house, jumping

Mastiffs aren't typically barky unless they have something to say.

Check It Out

SOLVING PROBLEM BEHAVIORS CHECKLIST

✓ Reinforce basic training with positive methods.
✓ Manage problem behaviors as soon as you recognize them.

✓ Consult the services of a professional trainer, animal behavior consultant, or veterinary behaviorist if you're unsure how to solve the problem yourself.
✓ Be persistent in solving the problem.

up, or nipping, take it seriously. If these behaviors are new, the first step is to take your dog to the veterinarian, as your Mastiff may have an underlying health issue that's causing the problem. Snap a photo or take a video of your dog in action. Show it to your veterinarian, as it may help during your explanation of the disruptive problem.

Barking

The Mastiff isn't a barky dog unless he really has something to say. With some Mastiff puppies, it takes two years and reaching maturity before they use their vocal cords to defend and protect their territory. Most of time, before even uttering a sound, he's apt to stand at attention, wrinkle his forehead, and think about his next move. When he finally does sound the two-woof alarm, it's usually out of excitement, during playtime, or to let you know that an unexpected visitor is on the premises. While you and your neighbors may not

mind the occasional bellow, non-stop howling and snarling when someone rings the doorbell, walks past the house, or delivers the mail annoys everyone.

Why do dogs bark too much? Some Mastiffs will bark if they're left alone for long hours. They become bored and lonely and may even suffer from separation anxiety.

How to Manage It

To stop your Mastiff from incessant barking:

• Figure out why he barks in the first place. If he's bored or lonely, give him additional exercise, some quality play time, or interesting toys to play with.
• Re-channel barking by teaching your Mastiff that remaining quiet pays bigger dividends than making noise. When he barks, catch the second or two when he stops. When he's quiet, quickly tell him "thank you" or "hush," and reward him with a food treat. Timing is key—don't

reward him until he has been quiet for a few seconds. Repeat several times a day until he catches on that "thank you" or "hush" means it's time to be quiet and earn a treat, while barking is not rewarded.

- Avoid yelling at your dog to stop barking, as this has the opposite effect and he's likely to think that you're reinforcing his behavior.

- Never use an electric shock collar, remote trainer, or e-collar (not to be confused with veterinary collars that protect incisions) on your dog, as these negative measures are cruel and abusive. While they may stun your dog and stop his barking for a few minutes, these collars use pain or fear and have dangerous side effects, such as increasing aggression.

- If the idea of having a watchdog was one of the reasons why you acquired a Mastiff in the first place, train your dog to alert you, but to stop barking when you give a cue. To do this, call him to you when he barks at someone at the door. When he complies, ask him to perform another behavior, such as sitting in front of you or fetching a toy before rewarding him. Resist the urge to calm your dog while he's barking by saying "OK" as this makes him think you approve of his behavior.

- Train your Mastiff not to bark when you are with him. If you're not there, don't expect him to learn on his own. For this reason, electronic devices that emit high frequency or loud sounds to deter barking may work once or twice, but are usually not effective in the long run.

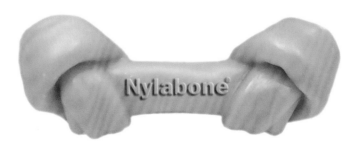

Stock up on a good supply of sturdy dog toys and Nylabones, and rotate them so your dog doesn't get bored with the same things all the time.

Chewing

All dogs are natural chewers. It begins when puppies are teething and need a way to exercise their jaws. This stage ends by age 2, but your Mastiff may still enjoy the habit. It makes sense that a dog with such strong jaws would want to keep munching. If he's gnawing on safe toys and sturdy bones that you give him, it's not a problem. But if he chews and destroys his bedding or your personal items, such as doors, furniture, clothing, electronics, or electrical wiring, he can injure himself and cause major damage to your home. Most veterinarians can tell horror stories about the strange items they have removed from Mastiff stomachs. One Mastiff even chewed through a baby gate.

You can't really blame your Mastiff for his oral destruction, as dogs don't know the difference between your cell phone and a Nylabone. To his way of thinking, if an object has an interesting taste, texture, or odor, it's fair game for chewing.

How to Manage It

To prevent your Mastiff from chewing your valuables, follow these tips:

- Create dog-safe zones in your home. Block off rooms that contain your precious items by closing the doors or placing baby gates over entrances. De-clutter the floors, tables, and counters. Pick up clothing, shoes, electronics, knick-knacks, children's toys, craft items, and important papers. Store them on high shelves or in locked cabinets or containers that your dog can't reach.
- Stock up on a good supply of sturdy dog toys and Nylabones, and rotate them so your dog doesn't get bored with the same things all the time. Leave a few in every area of your home that your dog visits. Other than jumbo-size Nylabone products or antler chews, you may have a hard time finding dog toys that a Mastiff can't destroy. New tough-chew products are becoming more readily available, so keep checking for them at pet supply stores and online pet stores.
- Supervise your dog with new toys. With a strong-chewing Mastiff, make sure he doesn't tear pieces off and swallow them. These can become lodged in his throat, and he can choke.
- Never leave your Mastiff unsupervised around household items you do not want him to chew. If you can't watch him, either for a few minutes or an hour or two, leave him in an exercise pen, crate, or dog-proof area with several of his favorite chew toys.
- To prevent boredom, provide plenty of exercise for your dog. A tired Mastiff is less likely to wreak havoc on his surroundings than one who lies on the couch all day.
- If you see your Mastiff chewing something he shouldn't, don't yell at him. Instead, offer a trade with an

Don't leave your dog unsupervised in the yard for long hours.

acceptable toy or a food treat. Say "Give," and when he drops the object to take the toy or food, pick up the object and say "Good boy!"

Digging

When you watch a Mastiff dig, there's no doubt that he's having the time of his life. His heart and soul goes into hitting rock bottom, and his powerful feet can displace hard-packed dirt faster than you can say "Whoa!" It's actually a joy to see all this activity—unless it means the demise of your newly planted lawn or expensive plants.

Dogs dig for several reasons. They're bored, frustrated, or want to bury their favorite bone. Some dogs like to hollow out a warm (or cool), comfy place to hang out. Others want to reach small mammals like moles or voles underground. Dogs have acute hearing, and they can actually hear them scurrying through underground burrows. Their keen sense of smell directs them to the exact spot to dig. Or, they may excavate just because

LATE BLOOMERS

Sensitive and intelligent, Mastiff puppies want to please you. They're quick learners, and it only takes a few words from you to direct their behavior in a positive manner. When puberty strikes at around nine months of age, think of your Mastiff as an unruly teenager. Mastiff puppies are late bloomers and can still act puppyish until two years of age. Throughout this time, your dog may challenge you by pushing the limits to see how much he can get away with before you stop whatever it is he wants to do.

To get through this phase:

• Be firm and consistent when giving commands.

• Never hit or shake your dog. Keep training positive.

• Provide plenty of exercise to help tire out your puppy.

• Redirect your puppy's attention with a game or interactive toys.

• Teach your puppy tricks or fun games to take his mind off getting into mischief.

• Schedule training sessions before meals or after a nap, when he's eager to learn.

• Keep training sessions brief—about 10 to 15 minutes at home and 30 to 45 minutes for classes.

• Don't correct your dog if you don't catch him in the act. He won't connect something he did earlier with your displeasure.

the soil has an interesting odor they want to paw at and investigate. Count on areas newly fertilized with chicken and steer manure to attract canine archaeologists.

While digging may look harmless, it can be dangerous if your dog reaches electrical wiring or tears a toenail if it catches on a sharp object.

How to Manage It
Identify what type of digger you are dealing with and take measures to prevent it:

• Dogs who dig out of boredom or frustration can benefit from having more interaction with you. Spend some quality time playing or exercising with your Mastiff. Take your dog for a walk in a new location for a minimum of 20 minutes once or twice a day.

• Try teaching him a few new tricks or games. The mental stimulation may divert his interest in digging.

- Don't leave your dog unsupervised in the yard for long hours. Hire a pet sitter or dog walker, or ask a neighbor or friend to visit your dog in your absence.
- To protect delicate yard areas, erect a small fence around the garden and install protective covers around all above- and underground wiring.
- Never put your dog outdoors on a hot day. Your Mastiff can't tolerate high temperatures. It's better to leave him indoors in an exercise pen if you must leave.
- To give your dog a place to stay cool on warm days, set up a child's small wading pool and fill with a few inches of water.
- Provide a shaded, grassy area for your dog to cool off.
- If you catch your dog in the act of digging, don't yell at him. He'll only resume when you're not around. Instead, interrupt him with a short, authoritative "No!" When he stops, offer him a food treat or a toy to reward him for stopping.
- To deter digging, cover bare patches in the yard with stones, tiles, wood, or chicken wire.
- Build a small digging area solely for your dog's pleasure. He'll appreciate a shady spot about 3 feet (1 m) wide, 6 feet (2 m) long, and 2 feet (.5 m) deep. To let your dog know that this spot is for him, let him see you bury one or two of his favorite bones a few inches beneath the dirt. Tell him to go get them. If he doesn't understand, dig them up yourself and make a big fuss over the fact. When he finds them, praise him lavishly.

Housesoiling

Once your puppy is completely housetrained and able to go outside on his own, cleaning up messes in the house should be a thing of the past. While you can probably tolerate the occasional accident if your dog doesn't have access to the yard or if he has a quick bout of diarrhea, repeated eliminations indoors may signal a problem. Solidly housetrained Mastiffs would rather urinate anywhere other than inside their own home.

How to Manage It

To figure out why your Mastiff is leaving puddles in the house:

- Take your dog to the veterinarian to make sure the inappropriate urination isn't the result of an underlying medical issue.

    –Bladder infections, stones, and tumors signal an urgency to urinate even when the bladder has only a small amount of urine.

    –Prostate gland disease in unneutered males and increased

water intake may also be the cause. The increased thirst may be the result of hormonal imbalances, kidney failure, liver diseases, and cortisone medications, such as prednisone.

   –Some spayed females may develop urinary incontinence and "leak" urine while they sleep, but it can be treated with medication or natural products.

   –Senior dogs begin to lose bladder control as they age, or they may suffer from cognitive dysfunction syndrome (CDS) (see Chapter 9), which causes the dog to lose the warning sensation of having to urinate or defecate.

- Once your dog receives a clean bill of health, redouble your housetraining process. Take him outside first thing in the morning, after meals, during playtime, and before bed. Keep an eye out for any signs that he wants to use the outdoors. If you can't watch your dog, put him in his exercise pen or crate. A room with newspapers may work, if he uses them.

- Evaluate what's happening in the household. Family upheaval or lack of order can trigger anxiety and lapses in housetraining.

- If a dog loses control of his bladder while greeting a visitor or a certain family member, this signals submissive urination and a loss of confidence, which is a behavior issue rather than a physical problem. To stop this behavior, build your dog's confidence by teaching him some tricks or asking him to perform sit, stay, or down behaviors before someone comes to visit. Ask guests or the family member to ignore the dog when they come in and to keep their greetings low-key. Although it's difficult, don't say anything to your dog when he urinates—simply clean it up. Above all, do not yell or punish him. Ignore the mistake and, with time and

Take your dog to the veterinarian to make sure the inappropriate urination isn't the result of an underlying medical issue.

patience, he'll eventually outgrow it.

- Sometimes males and even a few females may mark their territory in the house by urinating, especially if they have not been neutered or spayed. Studies show a sharp decrease in this activity following sterilization surgery. If you see your male begin to lift his leg, say, "No!" in a strong, firm voice and immediately usher him outdoors. Small-breed owners usually solve this problem by placing a cloth doggy bellyband or doggy diaper on their dog while he's in the house, but this may prove challenging with a Mastiff because of his giant size. These devices work on some dogs, once they begin to associate getting uncomfortably wet with remaining inside.

Above all, never banish your dog to the backyard all the time because of a few accidents. Take steps to figure out why there's a problem and solve it. Mastiffs are social butterflies and will suffer if isolated.

Jumping Up

Leave it to an energetic Mastiff to jump to greet you up close and personal. With a giant breed this can be a problem and should be discouraged. The dog outweighs a small child and some adults and can easily knock them over.

If you have a puppy, resist the urge to encourage jumping up while he's still small. He won't understand why you won't appreciate it when he's full-grown.

How to Manage It

Teaching your dog not to jump up isn't difficult. It just takes consistency. Here are a few tips:

- Sense when your dog is about to jump up and fold your arms over your chest. Without saying anything to him, turn your body away from him. Ignore him until he returns all four feet to the floor. Then praise him, but keep your applause low-key. If he jumps up again, repeat.
- Do not knee your dog in the chest, step on his back feet, grab his collar, yell at him, or push him down. This may work once or twice, but it won't solve the problem. He's jumping because he wants your attention, and these negative reactions reward that behavior.
- Instruct guests not to pet your dog if he tries to jump up on them, even if they say they don't mind. Tell them that you're training him and would appreciate their cooperation.
- Ask your dog to do something different before he jumps, such as "sit." Praise him when he complies.

Shyness

It's not unusual for some Mastiffs to lack confidence and act shy. The behavior problem is a combination of their genetic makeup—how their parents

Anytime you're dealing with a behavior problem that you can't solve, it's time to consult an expert.

and grandparents acted—and a lack of socialization as young puppies. Some Mastiffs require more socialization and early training than others. When they don't receive it, they are insecure whenever they leave the house. With a giant breed, this can become a problem if you take your dog to the veterinarian or go on an outing.

How to Manage It

To ease your dog's shyness and to build his confidence:

- Take him to obedience classes or dog sports, such as agility, rally, carting, or weight-pulling.
- Continue socializing him so he can meet a variety of people in different settings and experiences.

Nipping

Some Mastiffs like to use their teeth to give little love bites when playing. Don't tolerate this behavior, regardless of how harmless it may seem. Your dog may not understand that these love nips hurt and have the potential to cause serious injury to a small child or an adult. Some puppies act more bitey when they're tired, and they may need a nap if their play escalates. Other Mastiffs may nip if they don't want to do something, such as have their nails trimmed.

A study conducted by the National Council on Pet Population Study and Policy (NCPPSP) and published in the *Journal of Applied Animal Welfare Science* (JAAWS), revealed that biting is one of the top ten reasons why people take their dogs to animal shelters.

How to Manage It

- Resist yelling or physically punishing your dog as that only makes the problem worse.
- When your dog nips at your hand, say "Ouch!" which startles him into stopping, and put him in his crate for a short 10-minute time out.
- When you let him out, give him a toy to redirect him. If he bites again, let out a yelp like another dog would and crate him again for a slightly longer period of time—20 or 30 minutes. The message is that when he bites too hard, the interaction with you stops.
- If you feel overwhelmed and cannot stop the behavior, get some help. Before the problem escalates, contact an animal behaviorist or professional dog trainer who is experienced with giant breeds who bite.

When to Seek Professional Help

You've spent time and energy socializing and training your Mastiff, but for some reason your dog's behavior has gone awry and now he's unmanageable. Perhaps it began as a minor annoyance that has slowly built up into a serious problem. It may be nips that have turned into bites breaking the skin if the dog gets too close, or it may be that he's escalated from chewing up a little pillow to tearing up furniture, clothing, or anything else left lying around the house. Or, it may be that your dog grunted while eating if you or another dog approached his food bowl, but recently he's trying to bite.

Anytime you're dealing with a behavior problem that you can't solve, it's time to consult an expert. Some behavior problems, such as separation anxiety or aggression, are complicated and not easily solved by taking your dog to another obedience class.

Today, there are many people who call themselves professional dog trainers. Before hiring anyone, discuss their qualifications and experience with problem behaviors. To locate an animal behavior consultant, contact the International Association of Animal Behavior Consultants (IAABC) at www. iaabc.org. These professionals evaluate, manage, and work with owners to modify serious canine behaviors. The American

Q: What should I do about a Mastiff with separation anxiety?

A: The Mastiff who sticks to his owner like glue all the time and becomes anxious or has trouble when you leave may suffer from separation anxiety. Severe signs include hyperventilating, eliminating in the house, trying to escape, or having increased heart rate. If this is the case, consult with your veterinarian before trying to solve the problem on your own.

The second step is to begin independence training. Start with teaching your dog the down-stay while you stand across the room. The idea is to build your dog's confidence without putting him into a stressful situation. From there, build up to a down-stay with you going to another room. To release, don't call your dog to come to you. Instead, walk back to him.

Your dog should feel confident that you are only leaving him temporarily and that you'll return in a reasonable time.

Whenever you leave the house, give him a favorite chew toy or a food-stuffed puzzle toy to divert his attention. Provide vigorous exercise to help tire him out before your departure. Keep your goodbyes and return greetings low-key and matter-of-fact. Don't rush into the house and pay attention to him right away, either. Let him wait a minute or two, and keep calm. This sends the message that he's okay with or without you in the house.

—Vera Wikinson, Certified Dog Behavior Consultant and Certified Pet Dog Trainer with The Cooperative Dog in Brookline, Massachusetts

College of Veterinary Behaviorists (ACVB) certifies veterinary behaviorists and can help you locate a professional in your area (www.dacvb.org). These are medical experts who specialize in animal behavior.

Chapter
8

Activities With
Your Mastiff

If it's a choice between staying home alone or leaving the house with you, a Mastiff will run to the front door and give you a look that says, "Please take me along!" Whether you schedule a road trip, visit hospital patients, or attend agility classes with your Mastiff, a little planning will help make the experience memorable for you and your dog

Traveling With a Dog

If you want to include your Mastiff in your travel plans, make sure he's well socialized and accustomed to going out and about long before you leave. Otherwise, it may be a traumatic experience for him, especially if he suffers from motion sickness.

Car Travel

A road trip may be exciting to you, but for a Mastiff it's not such a thrill. While some dogs love car rides, others dread them because of prior bad experiences. And face it—how comfortable can a Mastiff really get in a bucket seat? Add the normal Mastiff drool factor to even more drool from anxiety, a too-warm interior, and motion sickness, and you could have a very unhappy giant dog on your hands.

Before hitting the open highway with your dog, take a few precautions to ensure his safety and comfort:

- **Practice rides.** Begin a few weeks earlier with several short trips so he becomes accustomed to the motion of the car. To avoid vomiting or an upset stomach, don't feed your dog for at least two hours prior to leaving.
- **Take supplies.** Pack a doggy bag with food, water, a backup leash and collar (in case one breaks), your dog's immunization record, and a pet emergency kit (see Chapter 9).
- **Buckle up.** On car rides of any length, even to the veterinarian, protect your Mastiff in case of an accident. In a 30 mph (48 km/h) collision, a dog can exert a force of up to 20 times his body weight. Place him in a well-secured crate or fit him with a well-designed doggy safety harness that buckles into the car seat belt. Barriers separating the passenger and driver's area may seem like a good idea, but they don't restrain your dog in case you have to jam on your brakes or are involved in an accident. A sudden stop can propel him through the windshield and out of the vehicle into oncoming traffic.
- **Restrict car jumping.** Don't let your Mastiff jump into the car on his own unless you drive a mini-van with a low doorway that your dog can easily step in and out of. A fall can cause serious injury to joints. Instead, attach a dog ramp or steps into the car or teach him how to put his front feet on the car seat by giving him the cue "Feet up." From there, you can give his back legs a boost into the car.

Check It Out

ACTIVITY PARTICIPATION CHECKLIST

✓ Socialize and train your dog before engaging in dog sports.

✓ Choose activities that a Mastiff can safely participate in without placing undue stress on his body.

✓ Prepare for traveling with your dog by researching dog-friendly accommodations and airline restrictions long before departure.

✓ Before leaving home, make sure that your dog is microchipped, and for backup, has current identification on his collar and that his collar fits properly. Take a second leash in case the first one breaks or gets lost.

✓ Keep a supply of poop bags in your car or dog bag. Always clean up and properly dispose of your dog's eliminations while out in public.

• **Don't leave him alone.** Never leave your dog alone in the car, especially in warm weather—even in the shade with the windows cracked. A study by the Stanford University School of Medicine showed that in 72°F (22°C) weather, a car's interior temperature heats up by 32° in the first 30 minutes. Mastiffs and other short-nosed and large or giant breeds quickly become overheated and can die if the temperature reaches 120°F (49°C). Battery-operated fans or cooling pads do little to keep a Mastiff cool.

• **Make frequent stops.** While driving long distances, give your dog bathroom breaks and a chance to stretch his legs every two or two hours. Puppies may need more frequent stops, but choose clean areas where other dogs have not frequented, to avoid the chance of

disease. Be sure to pick up and properly dispose of eliminations.

• **Bring food from home.** Carry enough food for your dog's trip, as a change in food can upset his system and cause diarrhea or vomiting.

• **Pack bottled water.** Always bring along plenty of water from home or bottled water, as a change in water can trigger intestinal upset and cause diarrhea.

• **Keep windows partially open.** When a dog hangs his head out the car window, it may look like he's having fun, but if a rock or debris flies into his eye it could injure him. If your dog is sitting next to the window, open it only enough so that he can't hang his head out the window.

Leaving on a Jet Plane
Today, flying the friendly skies on a

commercial airline, especially with a Mastiff, isn't so friendly. In fact, it has become more daunting than ever before, with endless rules for people and dogs. In some circumstances, flying a dog can be downright risky, and it should never be undertaken lightly. Strict regulations by the U.S. Department of Agriculture (USDA) dictate how pets are treated on airlines, but it's not a guarantee that a dog will arrive safely.

The ASPCA does not recommend flying your dog on a commercial flight, especially since a Mastiff must ride in an airline-approved crate in the cargo section. Most large jets cool, heat, and pressurize the cargo areas with the same system as the main cabin, but the heat/cooling system is often shut off during a delay when the plane is waiting to take off, to save fuel or power. At these times, dogs can quickly overheat. For this reason, some commercial airlines do not transport dogs during extreme hot and cold weather or accept dogs in cargo.

If you must relocate long distance and cannot transport your dog by car, contact the commercial airline in advance for its shipping restrictions, requirements, fees, and reservations. One general requirement is a health certificate from a veterinarian who has examined your dog within ten days of transportation. The American Kennel Club (AKC) website has a list of specific pet travel regulations for airline carriers at www.akc.org/pdfs/canine_legislation/airline_chart.pdf.

Currently, one airline has permanent embargoes on Mastiffs, and another will not accept Mastiffs if the temperature on any part of the flight is 75ºF (24ºC) or higher, so make sure you check before you book.

If you do fly your dog, always book a nonstop flight, avoid layovers and change of planes, and never tranquilize your Mastiff, as sedatives may have dangerous side effects at high altitudes.

When staying at pet-friendly lodging, always walk your dog on a leash while on the grounds.

SPORTS AND SAFETY

Before leaving home or getting started in any activities with your Mastiff, take a few precautions:

- Visit his veterinarian for an examination. Your dog's heart, lungs, and joints should be checked for any abnormalities that might exert his system during exercise.

- Have your dog microchipped, and register the chip with a national database. If your dog gets lost, the animal control officer, shelter, or veterinary clinic that finds him can scan for the chip and reunite you.

- Don't feed your dog for at least two hours before traveling or exercising.

- Always bring along plenty of fresh drinking water from home or purchase bottled water for your dog. Public water sources contain different chemicals that may upset his system and cause diarrhea.

- During hot weather camping and other outings, keep your dog cool and out of the sun by popping up a small tent or using a shade tarp. Include a small ice chest with bags of ice cubes.

Alternatively, consider hiring a charter airline company to fly you and your Mastiff to your destination, or book a reservation for your dog on a professional pet transporter, such as Pet Airways, a pet-only airline (www.petairways.com). All dogs, regardless of size, fly in the cabin, and pet attendants supervise the dogs' needs while in flight.

Pet-Friendly Lodging

When booking overnight accommodations, call ahead and inquire if the hotel, motel, or bed-and-breakfast permits dogs and specifically Mastiffs. Many establishments do not take big dogs, although more are changing their policies and welcoming any canine guests.

To find pet-friendly motels, hotels, or vacation rentals, access print and online listings, including Fido Friendly (www.fidofriendly.com) and Dog Friendly (www.dogfriendly.com). Be sure to ask about extra fees, as many places charge a pet deposit or cleaning fee, and ask where the designated doggy potty area is located.

Always follow this home-away-from-home etiquette:

- Always walk your dog on a leash while on the grounds.
- Don't let him jump on guests. Some people are frightened when they meet a Mastiff.
- Never leave your dog unattended in the room as he may feel lonely and bark or become destructive. If you must leave him for a short time, put him in his crate and make sure he doesn't disturb guests by making noise.
- Bring a few of his favorite toys, and don't let him chew anything in the room, such as the bedspread or furniture.

Sports and Activities

If your Mastiff seems content to hang out with you at the computer or go for a walk, but you're looking to spice things up a bit, there are many organized dog sports you can become involved in. Only purebred Mastiffs are eligible to compete at dog shows, but all Mastiffs may become involved in other activities. You can choose to participate occasionally or become competitive and earn AKC or United Kennel Club (UKC) titles. To encourage Mastiff owners to demonstrate their dogs' attributes and trainability, the Mastiff Club of America (MCOA) awards a Working Dog Certificate. To learn more about the program, check out the MCOA's website at www.mastiff.org.

Mastiffs possess a desire to please and because of their historic background

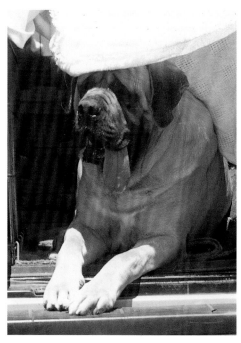

During hot weather outings, keep your dog cool and out of the sun by using a shade tarp.

are capable of succeeding in a variety of activities.

Agility

While a Mastiff might not be the fastest dog on the agility course, he's a hard worker and usually the most fun to watch. In agility, dogs maneuver up, over, and around obstacles, and are judged on speed and accuracy. Dogs scale an A-frame, climb a dogwalk, and run through a tunnel. From twisting around weave poles, jumping a few bars, and leaping through a suspended tire, dogs walk across a see-saw and pause on a table.

The challenge for all dogs is remaining on the course and completing all of the obstacles in the pattern chosen by the judge. Handlers help their dogs navigate the course as quickly as possible without errors. Dogs with the fewest point deductions and the fastest time may qualify for titles in three levels of competition: novice, open, and excellent.

Perfecting a performance takes time, patience, and positive training, but for the dogs, half the fun is getting out of the house and showing off what they can accomplish. For more information about agility, contact the AKC (www.akc.org) or the United States Dog Agility Association (www.usdaa.com).

AKC's Canine Good Citizen Program

Once your dog has mastered the training basics of sit, come, stay, down, and walk nicely on a leash, you might as well have him earn his AKC's Canine Good Citizen (CGC) award. Along with its pre-CGC program, called the STAR Puppy Program, it proves that your dog is a good citizen. For owners who want to become involved in therapy work with their Mastiffs, a CGC is often the first step toward qualifying. It also helps if you want to rent a home.

The CGC test consists of two parts. The first asks the owner to sign a Responsible Dog Owners' Pledge stating that the owner takes responsibility for his dog's health, safety, and quality of life, while not letting his dog infringe on the rights of others.

The second part consists of ten basic tests your dog must pass, which include his appearance and grooming; willingness to accept the approach of a stranger; ability to sit politely for petting, calm down after play or praise, walk on a loose leash, and walk through a crowd; successfully demonstration of the *sit*, *down*, *stay*, and *come* commands; reactions to other dogs and distractions; and behavior when left alone.

If your Mastiff can perform these tasks, you do not need to enroll in special classes. An AKC Canine Good Citizen (CGC) evaluator can administer the CGC test. Once your Mastiff passes with flying colors, he can add the CGC title to his name.

Carting

Throughout history Mastiffs have been used to transport goods across vast landscapes by pulling carts and wagons. Today, carting or drafting has become less a necessity and more of a popular way to show off the breed's willingness to help. Mastiffs who pull carts can participate in children's parades and haul gardening supplies. Drafting or carting is not about

When your puppy is four to six months old, he's ready to go for a short walk for one to two short blocks. By six to seven months of age, he can walk several blocks or up to 1 mile (1.5 km). At one year, he can handle a 2-mile (3-km) walk.

For the first two years, puppies should not go jogging with you or jump or run in organized canine sports. This places too much exertion on developing joints and limbs, which can cause injury and lead to crippling problems later in life.

how much weight your dog pulls, but rather how well the dog and handler can maneuver the cart. While most people refer to this activity as carting, titles earned during competition are called draft titles or draft tests.

Every year, the MCOA holds a drafting test at their national specialty gathering to demonstrate the breed's ability to work. It includes both obedience and drafting exercises, such as hitching, maneuvering, weight load, and distraction.

Conformation (Showing)

If your dog seems near-perfect, you may wish to participate in conformation, also known as dog showing. Mastiffs must be registered with a national club, such as the AKC, the UKC, or the Canadian Kennel Club (CKC), in order to compete. Dogs who are neutered or spayed or have an AKC limited registration cannot be shown in conformation. At a show, a judge will evaluate your dog in the show ring as to his temperament and how closely his

physical characteristics meet the breed standard, the written description of the ideal Mastiff.

Dog shows are very organized events with specific rules. To earn a championship and add the initials "Ch" before his name, your Mastiff must accumulate 15 points. For information on dog showing, check out the AKC website (www.akc.org).

You will need to train your dog to stand for the judge's examination and how to gait beside you in a straight line and around in a circle. Kennel clubs and private instructors teach conformation classes where you can learn the ins and outs of dog handling.

Junior Handling

With supervision, youngsters 9 to 18 years of age can show a Mastiff in junior showmanship at AKC and Mastiff Club national and regional specialties. This youth-oriented competition helps young handlers learn about dog shows and

At a show, a judge will evaluate your dog as to how closely he meets the breed standard.

develop their skills with their dogs.

Unlike conformation shows, in which the dog is solely judged on his breed characteristics, in junior showmanship, only the juniors' skills are evaluated. More than winning ribbons, this activity helps young people develop a strong bond with their dog. For more information, consult the AKC website (www.akc.org). Youngsters may also compete with their Mastiffs in other performance events.

Obedience

Obedience competitions measure how well a dog and handler can execute several tasks when directed by the judge. If your dog has already learned how to sit, stay, down, come, and walk nicely on a leash, add standing for the exam and heeling in a precise figure-8 pattern. Then it's lots of practice, practice, practice— with distractions—before most dogs are ready to compete.

The judge instructs the handler, and the handler must give the command to his dog only once. Three levels of competition for first-time and repeat competitors are available: Novice, Open, and Utility. All dogs begin with a perfect score of 200, and points are deducted for imperfections. The top scorer of the day is awarded the prestigious High in Trial (HIT). Dogs can earn Companion Dog (CD), Companion Dog Excellent (CDX), Utility (UD), and Utility Dog Excellent (UDX) titles. The Obedience Trial Champion (OTCH) is the ultimate obedience title.

Not only does earning an obedience title with your dog help build a bond between you, but the training proves invaluable at home and whenever you take your dog out in public.

Rally Obedience

Less structured than traditional obedience, rally requires dogs and handlers to perform a different exercise at 12 to 20 stations. Handlers read directions to follow basic commands such as sit, stay, or down, and incorporate turns and various speeds. Dog-and-handler teams must complete the timed course with a minimum of 70 points to achieve a qualifying score. To earn a Novice, Advanced, or Excellent title, dogs must earn three qualifying scores from two different judges.

If your Mastiff passes the CGC test, he may be a good candidate for a therapy dog.

KEEPING YOUR SENIOR FIT

Q: Can an older Mastiff use a stability ball to stay fit?

A: A stability ball can help a senior Mastiff stay flexible for exercise. Ball work helps provide core strength to the large muscles of the forelimbs, hindlimbs, and trunk. These areas often become compromised in large working breeds, such as the Mastiff. Physical therapy using a ball will also help improve balance and perception, which helps a senior dog navigate his environment. One of the first things that dogs lose later in life is balance and perception. The ball helps with endurance and stamina too, which is key to an older dog.

—Debbie Gross Saunders, DPT, MSPT, OSC, CCRP

Therapy Work

A visit from a Mastiff can raise anyone's spirits, let alone those of children or adults in a therapeutic setting. With a big nudge of his nose and an eagerness to accept pats and hugs, the Mastiff's outgoing personality and stature make him a natural at therapy work. Oozing oodles of charm, he lowers blood pressure, inspires activity, and improves social interaction in those around him. After a little training, a Mastiff can learn not to jump on the bed and to sit patiently for petting.

To train for therapy work, dogs need extensive socialization to people, places, and situations, and exposure to medical equipment is essential. If you're interested in volunteering with your dog at a nearby facility, contact them to learn about their requirements. For certification, contact Therapy Dogs International (www.tdi-dog.org) or the Delta Society (www.deltasociety.org).

The AKC Therapy Dog program awards a Therapy Dog (THD) title to dogs who have been certified by AKC-recognized therapy dog organizations.

With so many activities to keep you and your Mastiff busy, there's hardly time to laze around the house.

Chapter
9

Health of
Your Mastiff

With the right amount of a nutritious diet and regular exercise, your Mastiff will likely remain your loyal companion for ten years or more. Because he can't tell you when he's not feeling well, it's up to you to watch for signs of illness and to keep your Mastiff in tip-top shape.

Finding a Vet

Maintaining your Mastiff's health begins with choosing the right veterinarian. This professional utilizes the latest in veterinary advances and diagnostic testing to help your dog live a long and happy life.

To locate a knowledgeable veterinarian who feels comfortable treating a Mastiff, ask your breeder for a referral. If she doesn't live nearby or know any local veterinarians, try contacting other breeders or Mastiff owners who might be able to recommend someone. Ask the local kennel club, the regional Mastiff club, or other dog owners for names.

If you need a veterinary specialist, contact the American Veterinary Medical Association (AVMA) website (www.avma.org) and search "veterinary specialty organizations."

Annual Vet Visit

Like people, a Mastiff should have a checkup or wellness visit once a year until he becomes a senior at age six or seven. At that point, he'll need to see the veterinarian every six months. The exam can reveal problems you were unaware of or establish a baseline to measure any future changes.

During the exam, the veterinarian checks your dog to make sure that he is healthy. He'll measure your dog's weight, take his temperature, pulse, and respiration, and check his ears and eyes for signs of infection.

The veterinarian will check your Mastiff's body for the presence of any lumps, bumps, or red areas; examine his skin for any abnormalities; and look inside your dog's mouth for signs of gum disease. She may recommend drawing blood to check for heartworm, and will ask for a urine or stool sample to check for infections and parasites.

Vaccinations

Puppies need immunizations to guard against certain diseases. Core vaccines, such as rabies, distemper, parvovirus, and hepatitis should be given to all dogs, while noncore vaccines are only recommended for dogs whose lifestyle or environment puts them at risk. These include leptospirosis, coronavirus, tracheobronchitis, and Lyme disease.

While in the past dogs routinely received vaccinations once a year, the American Animal Hospital Association (AAHA) has issued new guidelines

Puppy Love

VACCINATION PROTOCOL

In their first weeks of life, puppies receive temporary immunity from certain diseases from their mother. This lasts for 8 to 14 weeks. When it begins to decline, puppies need protection from a series of core vaccines. These should be given at least 3 to 4 weeks apart.

The American Veterinary Medical Association (AVMA) recommends these vaccines, but always consult with your veterinarian.

Age	Vaccine
5 weeks	Parvovirus.
6 & 9 weeks	Combination vaccine (CAV-2), including adenovirus-2 cough and hepatitis, distemper, and parvovirus without leptospirosis*; parainfluenza (CPIV).
12 weeks or older	Rabies.
12 & 15 weeks	Combination vaccine; leptospirosis if traveling to an area where it occurs or where it is a concern; coronavirus where it is a concern; Lyme if it is a concern or if traveling to an area where it occurs.
After 15 weeks	Some puppies may need additional parvovirus vaccines, but ask your veterinarian.

*Note: Leptospirosis vaccine can cause adverse reactions in young puppies, so many veterinarians recommend waiting until the puppy is older to administer it.

Spaying and neutering prevent pregnancy and reduce and eliminate certain health and behavioral problems, including marking and aggression.

recommending vaccination once every three years and booster shots every three years. Before vaccinating your dog, discuss the recommended protocols in your area with your veterinarian. Adults no longer need yearly boosters.

Spaying and Neutering

Mastiffs who show in conformation cannot be spayed or neutered. Dogs who are not destined for the show ring should be neutered (males) or spayed (females). These procedures prevent pregnancy and reduce and eliminate certain health and

behavioral problems, including marking and aggression.

When to do it? Veterinarians once advised performing the operation before a female's first heat cycle, around six to eight months of age, but new research reveals potential health risks with spaying or neutering before puberty. These include prostatic cancer in males and increased risks of cranial cruciate ligament ruptures, bone cancer, and hip dysplasia. The chances are greater for obesity, diabetes, urinary tract infections, urinary incontinence, and hypothyroidism. Today, waiting to perform sterilization until the Mastiff reaches maturity at 18 to 36 months of age is recommended.

Parasites

No one likes a parasite. These freeloading pests plague dogs and threaten their health and comfort. They introduce bacteria and disease and can make you and your dog's life miserable. To rid your Mastiff of parasitic infestations, routine veterinary care is necessary.

Internal Parasites

Internal parasites live inside your dog and can cause a serious problem before you even realize your Mastiff has them. They siphon away nutrients your dog needs, and they can transmit disease.

Dogs come in contact with internal

parasites in a variety of ways, including being born with them, through insect bites, through contact with infected rodent feces, or by ingesting eggs or larvae. Symptoms include diarrhea, weight loss, anemia, dry hair, and vomiting. If you notice any of these signs, take your Mastiff to the veterinarian immediately for diagnosis and treatment.

Heartworms

One of the most dangerous internal parasites, heartworms grow up to 12 inches (30 cm) long and live in a dog's heart and the surrounding blood vessels. Heartworm larvae are transmitted to the dog by the bite of an infected mosquito. Symptoms may include lethargy, weight loss, coughing, and abnormal breathing, but most dogs do not show signs of infection. Heartworm is diagnosed by a blood test and an x-ray or ultrasound. The infestation can be treated, but it is often deadly. This disease can be prevented through daily or monthly chewable tablets of ivermectin and milbemycin oxime, which kills larvae in the bloodstream.

Hookworms

These small, thin worms are common canine parasites. Dogs become infected orally or through skin penetration. These dangerous life-threatening parasites stick to the wall of the small intestine, where they suck blood, mate, and expel their eggs through the dog's stool. Hookworm infestation produces symptoms of bloody to tar-like diarrhea, resulting in blood loss, weakness, malnutrition, sudden collapse, and death. Dogs of all ages are susceptible, but puppies are at high risk of infection. The larvae thrive in hot climates with high

Check It Out

HEALTH CHECKLIST

✓ Choose a qualified veterinarian you can talk to.

✓ Take your dog for a checkup once a year.

✓ Provide core vaccines and adult boosters without overvaccinating your Mastiff.

✓ Use parasite preventives only as needed.

✓ Watch for signs of illnesses and obtain treatment.

✓ Consider alternative treatments in addition to traditional veterinary care.

✓ Mastiffs are considered seniors at six or seven years of age and may need special care at that time.

Roundworms mostly affect puppies.

soft, watery stools, followed by expelling worms that resemble long strands of spaghetti either in their stool or vomit. Repeat dosages of deworming medication rid the dog's body of these worms. When you buy a puppy from a conscientious breeder, she should give you the dates when deworming medications were given. Many flea control products include roundworm protection.

humidity. Picking up pet waste promptly and keeping concrete areas clean and disinfected with a bleach solution helps prevent contamination. Worming medication eradicates the worms.

Roundworms

The most common of the canine internal parasites, roundworms live in the digestive tract and mostly affect puppies, although a Mastiff can acquire them at any age. Mothers pass roundworm eggs to their puppies in the womb or during nursing. Dogs ingest roundworm larvae by eating a small rodent or bird that is carrying developing worms. Eggs also live in contaminated soil.

Five-week-old Mastiff puppies with roundworms will have a rounded, potbellied appearance, a dull coat, and

Whipworms

These parasites are recognized by their whip-like appearance. Whipworms dwell in the large intestine or at the meeting of the small and large intestine, known as the cecum. If your Mastiff ingests food, water, or dirt contaminated with whipworm eggs, he's likely to become infected. The eggs can live for 1 to 3 months until maturity. After hatching, they thrive on the blood supply and lay eggs, which pass through the feces.

Signs of whipworms include weight loss and anemia, with severe cases leading to intestinal hemorrhaging. Deworming medications help control whipworms, although some heartworm preventative products are also effective against whipworms. Cleaning up feces every day helps prevent infestation, although soil replacement from an uninfected area is the most effective prevention.

External Parasites

Fleas, ticks, mites, and ringworm (a fungal infection) live on your dog's skin and wreak havoc on your dog's life. Prevention is the key to controlling these troublemakers.

Fleas

Nothing is more annoying to dogs and people than fleas. One bite from these six-legged wingless insects causes skin irritation and scratching. If a Mastiff happens to be allergic to fleas, he'll tear and bite at his coat to relieve the discomfort until there are bare patches. Apart from causing your dog distress, fleas feed on the blood of their hosts and compromise the immune system. They lead to debilitation in adult dogs, and can transmit tapeworm infection. Flea allergy dermatitis (FAD) is the most common veterinary dermatological condition.

Slightly smaller than a sesame seed, fleas can jump incredible distances—from the ground to a dog's back—and they burrow in and out of a dog's skin. Although they have a short life cycle lasting from 2 weeks to 8 months, they can lay as many as 50 eggs a day.

Your dog does not have to live with these pests, as flea preventives that are safe, easy, and effective to use are available

Check your dog for fleas and ticks after he's been outside.

from veterinarians. If you prefer to use a natural remedy to ward off fleas and mosquitoes, try applying essential oils. A combination of lavender, peppermint, and lemongrass rubbed into a dog's coat can be effective and will give your Mastiff a pleasant odor. Be sure to repeat it twice a day, as it wears off. It helps to wash your dog's bedding in hot water once a week to prevent infestation.

Mites

Microscopic mites belong to the arachnid family and are highly contagious. The common types infest dogs' skin, ears, and nasal passages and cause severe itching and irritated skin. The veterinarian may perform a skin scraping to detect mites, and she can then prescribe treatment.

Ringworm

A fungus, rather than a worm, this external parasite is usually found in hot and humid climates. It is transmitted through direct contact with an infected animal or with ringworm spores. Ringworm causes round, hairless lesions and scaly skin, and is contagious to other dogs and people. The veterinarian will use an ultraviolet lamp (black light) to detect ringworm and will place a skin sample from the lesion under a microscope. To kill 80 percent of ringworm spores on surfaces, including your dog's crate and kennel area, apply a solution of 1 part bleach to 10 parts water.

Ticks

Resembling spiders, ticks pose serious health risks to dogs. From their lookouts on low-hanging plants and tall grasses, ticks sense an approaching host. They leap to attach themselves to a dog's head, neck, ears, or feet and begin feeding. Ticks can transmit Lyme disease, Rocky Mountain spotted fever, ehrlichiosis, tularemia, and babesiosis.

After exercising in a heavily wooded area, examine your Mastiff for ticks. Remove the entire tick carefully with tweezers and avoid handling it with your bare hands so the infectious agents do not enter your skin. Clean the area on your dog with hydrogen peroxide, alcohol, or soap and water. Kill the tick by dropping it into a container of alcohol before flushing it down the toilet. If you live in an area where Lyme disease is prevalent, talk to your veterinarian about the Lyme vaccination. Many tick repellents are also available from your veterinarian.

Breed-Specific Illnesses

Mastiffs are relatively healthy dogs, but like all breeds, they are not free from their share of hereditary health issues and genetic diseases. The Mastiff Club of America (MCOA) and conscientious Mastiff breeders recognize these medical

Mastiffs are relatively healthy dogs, but like all breeds, they are not free from their share of hereditary health issues and genetic diseases.

issues and work to eliminate or reduce the incidence of these diseases. They test adult dogs for genetic problems prior to breeding, and they moderate environmental factors, such as exercise and diet, which can affect bones and joints. Mastiffs who undergo health tests are listed at the Canine Health Information Center (CHIC) website (www. caninehealthinfo.org).

Cancer

Like many large breeds, cancer has become the most prevalent disease in Mastiffs. According to the MCOA's Health Survey, the major cause of death in Mastiffs is cancer. The most common cancers affecting Mastiffs are osteosarcoma (bone cancer), lymphoma, hemangiosarcoma, and mast cell tumors, with osteosarcoma the most common type of cancer in the breed. The MCOA helps provide Mastiff owners with research information about the disease and is gathering DNA from blood samples on all Mastiffs to help with research.

The ten early warning signs of cancer are:

1. Weight loss
2. Offensive odor
3. Loss of appetite
4. Sores that do not heal
5. Difficulty eating or swallowing
6. Persistent lameness or stiffness
7. Hesitation to exercise or loss of stamina
8. Difficulty breathing, urinating, or defecation
9. Bleeding or discharge from any body opening
10. Abnormal swellings that persist or continue to grow

If you notice any of these symptoms, take your Mastiff to his veterinarian immediately for an examination and diagnosis. Today, many advances in cancer research are improving the level of care and can sometimes help survival rates.

Cruciate Ligament Rupture

Like athletes, Mastiffs can injure and blow out their knees, although in dogs, many cruciate ligament ruptures are due to a gradual weakening or degeneration of the ligament. Bearing too much weight while bones are developing during puppyhood and obesity in adults often causes ruptured ligaments. Falling on a slippery surface or stumbling on a fast turn while running may also damage the knee.

When a dog ruptures his cruciate ligament, he will usually hold the affected leg off the ground and appear lame. The knee may swell, and you may hear a clicking noise in the knee when the dog walks. To diagnose the injury, your veterinarian can X-ray the knee and recommend surgery to correct the problem.

Cystinuria

Along with 60 other breeds, Mastiffs can suffer from painful cystinuria, a genetic kidney defect. A positive urinalysis proves the presence of cystine in the urine. A nitroprusside urine test performed at the University of Pennsylvania can also confirm cystine.

Cystinuria causes rare cystine stones to form in the kidneys and urinary tract, because of acidic rather than alkaline urine. When these stones and smaller crystals pass through the urinary tract, they may block it and cause extreme pain. Dogs with cystinuria may require emergency treatment to remove the stones.

To treat this condition and to keep the urine diluted, it is important that dogs drink plenty of fresh water throughout the day and night and have ample opportunity to urinate. The water bowl should be changed several times a day, and extra water should be added to food.

Your Mastiff's diet and treats should avoid salt, as this increases acidic urine and forms stones. Check with

Along with 60 other breeds, Mastiffs can suffer from painful cystinuria, a genetic kidney defect.

your veterinarian before giving any supplements, such as vitamin C or cranberry juice, as these decrease the pH level of the urine, which can encourage cystine stone formation. High levels of stress, or becoming overheated or dehydrated, may form stones as well. Your veterinarian may prescribe medication to help treat this condition.

Elbow Dysplasia

When the bones and cartilage of the elbow fail to fit together properly, it causes pain. An inherited condition, both genes and environment contribute to the development of elbow dysplasia. It affects young, rapidly growing dogs and causes pain, inflammation, and arthritis in the cartilage. A veterinarian can use computerized tomography (CT scan) or a series of X-ray views of different angles of the elbow joint to diagnose elbow dysplasia. Surgery is needed to correct the problem.

Epilepsy

Seizure disorders, or a temporary dysfunction of the brain, affect Mastiffs as well as many mixed and purebred dogs. During a seizure, the dog may jerk or become anxious, and he may salivate or lose bladder or bowel control. While upsetting to the owner, the dog does not feel any pain during a seizure and it is not life-threatening.

If a Mastiff suffers a seizure, a veterinarian should perform an examination to rule out other causes. Epilepsy is difficult to diagnose since other medical issues, such as hypothyroidism, may produce seizures. To date, no screening test is available to detect epilepsy. Severe cases of epilepsy can be controlled with medication, and some owners of epileptic dogs claim that feeding a raw diet reduces the incidence of seizures.

Hip Dysplasia

Hip dysplasia is an inherited abnormal development of the hip joint, in which the head of the thigh bone (femur) doesn't fit tightly into the hip socket. The loose fit causes inflammation and is the most common inherited orthopedic disease in dogs and the number one reason for rear-end lameness in many large breeds. It usually develops by 9 to 12 months of age. The signs include limping or a bunny-hop gait, and difficulty jumping or rising after a nap. Surgery is the only way to correct the misalignment.

Progressive Retinal Atrophy (PRA) and Canine Multifocal Retinopathy (CMR)

Both progressive retinal atrophy (PRA) and canine multifocal retinopathy (CMR) are inherited diseases of the retina that cause loss of vision and blindness in

HEALTH CERTIFICATIONS

To prevent some genetic health issues, conscientious Mastiff breeders perform the following health tests before breeding:

- Urine test after 18 months of age, by the University of Pennsylvania.

- Eye clearance after 2 years of age; exam must be repeated yearly.

- Heart certification after 1 year of age.

- Hip and elbow X-rays after 2 years of age.

- Thyroid panel.

Mastiffs and in many mixed-breed and purebred dogs. The early signs of PRA include dilated pupils and increased "eye shine," which coincides with night blindness. In advanced PRA, all light levels are affected and blindness ensues usually within 1 year of diagnosis. A dog with PRA will want to remain in well-lit areas. There is no cure and no medical treatment for PRA, but supplementing with antioxidants may slow the deterioration of the retina and delay the onset of blindness.

A veterinary ophthalmologist can diagnose PRA by dilating a dog's pupils with eye drops and examining the eye with an ophthalmoscope. Dogs with PRA should not be bred. A DNA blood test is available to determine if dogs are likely affected with PRA or are carriers. When you buy a puppy from a breeder, ask to see proof that both parents have been tested for and proven free of PRA.

Canine multifocal retinopathy (CMR) develops in puppies before four months of age and progresses slowly; the disorder might appear to heal, return, or possibly go away again. Some dogs with CMR may not show signs of this disease until later in life. Early signs include circular patches and gray-, tan-, or pink-colored lesions in the retina that resemble blisters.

Dogs with CMR should not be bred. The presence of this gene mutation is detected with a DNA sample, which can be done at any age, including in puppies. The results will not change later in life.

General Illnesses

Despite feeding your Mastiff a quality diet and providing the right amount of exercise, no breed is immune to illness at some point in life. Observing your dog for signs of illness in the early stages will

help identify a problem so you can obtain treatment and ease his symptoms.

Allergies

Like people, dogs are not immune to allergies. The most common allergens are pollens, molds, specific foods, and flea saliva. Allergy-producing substances enter a dog's system through breathing, eating, bites, and skin contact. Dogs react to allergens by wheezing, skin irritation, and itching. To diagnose an allergic reaction, take your dog to the veterinarian. She may use a blood test or skin test to screen for antibodies that produce common allergies. Seasonal allergies or ingredients in your dog's diet may be responsible for problems. Natural anti-inflammatory drugs and fatty acid supplements can help reduce allergic reactions.

Gastric Dilatation Volvulus (GDV) (Bloat)

A life-threatening emergency, bloat occurs in many large, deep-chested breeds. It occurs when the stomach expands with gas or fluids and twists, which prevents the gas or fluids from escaping. The expansion puts pressure on vital organs and impairs breathing. Emergency surgery is required immediately. Sometimes veterinarians may recommend surgery to reposition the stomach (gastropexy) and suture it to prevent future twisting.

Signs of bloating include a swollen or distended belly, rapid or shallow breathing, retching or vomiting without anything produced, restlessness, pale gums, and salivation. A dog may try to hide in a corner or want to be left alone.

If you suspect that your dog has bloat, even in the middle of the night, take him to the emergency clinic immediately. It may mean the difference between life and death.

Alternative Therapies

In addition to or in place of the conventional or traditional treatment offered by many veterinarians, many owners will obtain alternative therapies

Ask the Expert

Q: What is TCVM?

A: The treatment of many diseases seen in Mastiffs can be supplemented with traditional Chinese veterinary medicine (TCVM). There are five branches of TCVM. Acupuncture can help relieve pain from arthritis, and hip and elbow dysplasia. Herbal medicine and food therapy are useful in dealing with epilepsy and skin problems. *Tuina* is a wonderful massage technique to relieve tension and sore muscles. *Qigong* helps calm and stabilize the patient.

TCVM is becoming more available to supplement Western medicine in the treatment of many diseases. Customized food therapy can clear excess damp and heat contributing to skin diseases or build up deficient conditions. Acupuncture and herbal medicines can relieve pain associated with dysplasia or arthritis and balance the body to help control epilepsy and some eye conditions. Check www.IVAS.org or www.TCVM.com for a certified veterinarian near you.

—Deborah Mathis, DVM, CVA

for their Mastiff. Some alternative treatments, known as complementary and alternative veterinary medicine (CAVM), have been in existence for thousands of years. Many veterinarians add these therapies to their practices or may specialize in them. The AVMA offers guidelines for their use.

These treatments may include acupuncture, chiropractic, massage, herbals (including natural supplements, vitamins, and minerals), and homeopathy.

First-Aid Kit

You never know when disaster will strike. Having a canine first-aid kit easily accessible at home and in your car may save your dog's life. You can purchase a ready-made pet first-aid kit or assemble one yourself.

Once a year, freshen up and restock these supplies:

- **Animal Poison Control Center phone number**: 888-4ANI-HELP (888-426-4435). There may be a fee for the call. Use it if you think your dog has ingested poison.
- **Antacid tablets**: for upset stomach.
- **Antibacterial ointment**: apply to wounds after cleansing.
- **Antidiarrheal over-the-counter remedy**: to ease diarrhea symptoms.
- **Antihistamines**: to counter allergic reactions.

- **Cotton balls**: for cleansing wounds with solution.
- **Digital thermometer**: use rectally to monitor your dog's temperature.
- **Gauze**: for wrapping wounds or muzzling your dog.
- **Hydrogen peroxide (3%)**: used topically as a disinfectant to cleanse wounds; internally to induce vomiting if your dog has ingested poison. Consult with your veterinarian or poison control center before using.
- **Large syringe without needle or eyedropper**: to administer liquid medication.
- **Leash, harness, or blanket**: to help transport your dog if he is unable to walk.
- **Pet first-aid handbook**: for quick instructions until you contact the veterinarian.
- **Sterile saline eyewash**: to remove debris.
- **Towels or strips of clean cloth**: to control bleeding or protect wounds.
- **Vet Wrap**: stock 6 to 12 rolls of this self-sticking bandage.
- **Veterinarian's phone number and address**: include the nearest emergency veterinary clinic information.
- **Your dog's name, date of birth, and medical history**: aids the veterinarian when treating your dog.

Senior Dogs

Mastiffs become senior citizens at six or seven years of age. Fortunately, the 21st century is making it easier than ever before for Mastiffs to live longer and enjoy a better quality of life. If you observe signs of aging, such as increased thirst, more frequent urination or loose stools, loss of appetite, reduced mobility, or lethargy, notify your veterinarian. An annual wellness examination can spot the changes of aging early on.

Many dogs develop cognitive dysfunction syndrome (CDS) as they age. Signs of this canine version of Alzheimer's disease include aimless wandering, staring at walls, and confusion. Medication is available in some cases, although antioxidants can help older dogs with cognitive dysfunction. Taking your dog on a few short walks every day, learning a few new tricks, and playing with toys also helps keep senior dogs engaged in life around them.

Living with a Mastiff is always interesting. You will never forget the time you share with him and all of the pleasures he adds to your life. Above all, he provides loyalty and companionship and depends on you to care for him to the end of his days.

Resources

Associations and Organizations

Breed Clubs

American Kennel Club (AKC)
8051 Arco Corporate Drive, Suite 100
Raleigh, NC 27617-3390
Telephone: (919) 233-9767
Fax: (919) 233-3627
E-Mail: info@akc.org
www.akc.org

Canadian Kennel Club (CKC)
200 Ronson Drive, Suite 400
Etobicoke, Ontario M9W 5Z9
Telephone: (416) 675-5511
Fax: (416) 675-6506
E-Mail: information@ckc.ca
www.ckc.ca

Federation Cynologique Internationale (FCI)
Secretariat General de la FCI
Place Albert 1er, 13
B – 6530 Thuin
Belgique
www.fci.be

The Kennel Club
1 Clarges Street, Piccadilly
London
W1J 8AB
Telephone: 0844 463 3980
Fax: 0207 518 1028
www.the-kennel-club.org.uk

Mastiff Club of America (MCOA)
www.mastiff.org

United Kennel Club (UKC)
100 E. Kilgore Road
Kalamazoo, MI 49002-5584
Telephone: (269) 343-9020
Fax: (269) 343-7037
E-Mail: pbickell@ukcdogs.com
www.ukcdogs.com

Pet Sitters

National Association of Professional Pet Sitters
15000 Commerce Parkway, Suite C
Mt. Laurel, New Jersey 08054
Telephone: (856) 439-0324
Fax: (856) 439-0525
E-Mail: napps@petsitters.org
www.petsitters.org

Pet Sitters International
201 East King Street
King, NC 27021-9161
Telephone: (336) 983-9222
Fax: (336) 983-5266
E-Mail: info@petsit.com
www.petsit.com

Rescue Organizations and Animal Welfare Groups

American Humane Association (AHA)
1400 16th Street NW, Suite 360
Washington, D.C. 20036
Telephone: (800) 227-4645
www.americanhumane.org

American Society for the Prevention of Cruelty to Animals (ASPCA)
424 E. 92nd Street
New York, NY 10128-6804
Telephone: (212) 876-7700
www.aspca.org

Royal Society for the Prevention of Cruelty to Animals (RSPCA)
RSPCA Enquiries Service
Wilberforce Way, Southwater,
Horsham, West Sussex RH13 9RS
United Kingdom
www.rspca.org.uk

Sports
International Agility Link (IAL)
85 Blackwall Road
Chuwar Qld 4306, Australia
E-Mail: steve@agilityclick.com
www.agilityclick.com/~ial

North American Dog Agility Council (NADAC)
24605 Dodds Road
Bend, OR 97701
www.nadac.com

Therapy

Pet Partners
875 124th Ave, NE, Suite 101
Bellevue, WA 98005
Telephone: (425) 679-5500
Fax: (425) 679-5539
E-Mail: info@petpartners.org
www.petpartners.org

Therapy Dogs Inc.
P.O. Box 20227
Cheyenne WY 82003
Telephone: (877) 843-7364
Fax: (307) 638-2079
E-Mail: therapydogsinc@qwestoffice.net
www.therapydogs.com

Therapy Dogs International (TDI)
88 Bartley Road
Flanders, NJ 07836
Telephone: (973) 252-9800
Fax: (973) 252-7171
E-Mail: tdi@gti.net
www.tdi-dog.org

Training
Association of Professional Dog Trainers (APDT)
104 South Calhan Street
Greenville, SC 29601
Telephone: (800) PET-DOGS
Fax: (864) 331-0767
E-Mail: information@apdt.com
www.apdt.com

International Association of Animal Behavior Consultants (IAABC)
565 Callery Road
Cranberry Township, PA 16066
E-Mail: info@iaabc.org
www.iaabc.org

National Association of Dog Obedience Instructors (NADOI)
7910 Picador Drive
Houston, TX 77083-4918
www.nadoi.org

Veterinary and Health Resources
Academy of Veterinary Homeopathy (AVH)
P. O. Box 232282
Leucadia, CA 92023-2282
Telephone: (866) 652-1590
Fax: (866) 652-1590
www.theavh.org

American Academy of Veterinary Acupuncture (AAVA)
P.O. Box 1058
Glastonbury, CT 06033
Telephone: (860) 632-9911
Fax: (860) 659-8772
www.aava.org

American Animal Hospital Association (AAHA)
12575 W. Bayaud Ave.
Lakewood, CO 80228
Telephone: (303) 986-2800
Fax: (303) 986-1700
E-Mail: info@aahanet.org
www.aahanet.org

American College of Veterinary Internal Medicine (ACVIM)
1997 Wadsworth Blvd., Suite A
Lakewood, CO 80214-5293
Telephone: (303) 231-9939
Telephone (US or Canada): (800) 245-9081
Fax: (303) 231-0880
Email: ACVIM@ACVIM.org
www.acvim.org

American College of Veterinary Ophthalmologists (ACVO)
P.O. Box 1311
Meridian, ID 83860
Telephone: (208) 466-7624
Fax: (208) 466-7693
E-Mail: office13@acvo.org
www.acvo.org

American Holistic Veterinary Medical Association (AHVMA)
P. O. Box 630
Abingdon, MD 21009-0630
Telephone: (410) 569-0795
Fax: (410) 569-2346
E-Mail: office@ahvma.org
www.ahvma.org

American Veterinary Medical Association (AVMA)
1931 North Meacham Road, Suite 100
Schaumburg, IL 60173-4360
Telephone: (800) 248-2862
Fax: (847) 925-1329
E-Mail: avmainfo@avma.org
www.avma.org

ASPCA Animal Poison Control Center
Telephone: (888) 426-4435
www.aspca.org

British Veterinary Association (BVA)
7 Mansfield Street
London
W1G 9NQ
Telephone: 0207 636 6541
Fax: 0207 908 6349
E-Mail: bvahq@bva.co.uk
www.bva.co.uk

Canine Eye Registration Foundation (CERF)
P.O. Box 199
Rantorl, IL 61866-0199
Telephone: (217) 693-4800
Fax: (217) 693-4801
E-Mail: CERF@vmbd.org
www.vmdb.org

Orthopedic Foundation for Animals (OFA)
2300 NE Nifong Blvd
Columbus, Missouri 65201-3856
Telephone: (573) 442-0418
Fax: (573) 875-5073
Email: ofa@offa.org
www.offa.org

US Food and Drug Administration Center for Veterinary Medicine (CVM)
7519 Standish Place
HFV-12
Rockville, MD 20855
Telephone: (240) 276-9300 or (888) INFO-FDA
http://www.fda.gov/cvm

Publications

Books

Anderson, Teoti. *The Super Simple Guide to Housetraining.* Neptune City: TFH Publications, 2004.

Anne, Jonna, with Mary Straus. *The Healthy Dog Cookbook: 50 Nutritious and Delicious Recipes Your Dog Will Love.* UK: Ivy Press Limited, 2008.

Dainty, Suellen. *50 Games to Play With Your Dog.* UK: Ivy Press Limited, 2007.

Magazines

AKC Family Dog
American Kennel Club
260 Madison Avenue
New York, NY 10016
Telephone: (800) 490-5675
E-Mail: familydog@akc.org
www.akc.org/pubs/familydog

AKC Gazette: Digital Edition
American Kennel Club
260 Madison Avenue
New York, NY 10016
www.akc.org/pubs/gazette/digital_edition.cfm

Websites

Nylabone
www.nylabone.com

TFH Publications, Inc.
www.tfh.com

Index

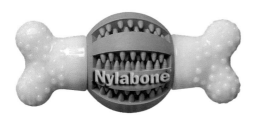

hookworms, 123–124
The Hound of the Baskervilles
(Doyle), 15
house-soiling behaviors, 100–102
house-training Mastiffs, 83–84

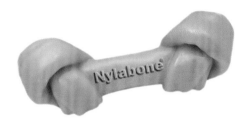

I

identification considerations, 41–42
International Association of Animal
Behavior Consultants (IAABC), 104

J

*Journal of the American Veterinary
Medical Association*, 40
jumping behaviors, 102
junior handling (activity), 114–115

L

Las Meninas (Velasquez), 15
leash training, 89
leash types (supplies), 42–43
lodging, pet-friendly, 111–112
Lyme Hall Mastiffs, 15

M

Mason (famous Mastiff), 14
Mastiff Club of America (MCOA),
10–11, 18, 112
media, Mastiffs in, 14–15
minerals (feeding), 49
mites, 126
Modern Family (TV show), 15
movement (physical characteristic),
21

N

nail care (grooming), 41, 72–73
neutering, spaying and, 122
nipping behaviors, 103–104
non-commercial food options,
54–56
Nylabone, 43, 97

O

obedience
activities, 115–116
training basics, 85–89
obesity (feeding), 58–59
origins of Mastiffs, 8–9
osteochondritis desiccans (OCD), 56

P

parasites, 38, 122–126
personality (characteristic), 21–22
pet-friendly lodging, 111–112
physical limitations, 25–26
positive training, 77
problem behaviors
barking, 95–96
chewing, 97–98

digging, 98–100
house-soiling, 100–102
jumping up, 102
nipping, 103–104
seeking help, 104–105
separation anxiety, 105
shyness, 102–103
professional help (behaviors),
104–105
progressive retinal atrophy (health
care), 129–130
proteins (feeding), 47–48
puppies
characteristics, 29–31
crate training, 82–83
food considerations, 38–39, 47, 56
grooming, 72
house-training, 83–84
puppy proofing, 37
socializing, 78–81
vaccinating, 120–122
walking, 25–26
weight considerations, 20

Photo Credits

Dedication

Acknowledgments

Special thanks for sharing their dedication and expertise to Betsy Harvey, Pat Flanagan Borracci, Dr. William R. Newman, Charles Cuthbert, Margo Lauritsen, Nicki Camerra, Vera Wilkinson, Debbie Gross Saunders, DPT, MSPT, OSC, CCRP, and Deborah Mathis, DVM, CVA. My appreciation also to my editors Stephanie Fornino and Heather Russell-Revesz for their patience and wisdom.

About the Author

Elaine Waldorf Gewirtz writes articles and books about human and canine behavior, care, and health, and is a multiple recipient of the prestigious Maxwell Award from the Dog Writers Association of America (DWAA) and the ASPCA Humane Issues Award. She is the author of *American Pit Bull Terriers* and *Bichons Frises* (Animal Planet™ Pet Care Library) and *Boston Terrier* (DogLife). Elaine and her husband live in Westlake Village, California, with their four-footed best friends.

Nylabone®

Safe, Healthy Chewing
Since 1955

Nylabone® treats and dog chews are designed to meet the various chewing styles and strengths of every size and breed of dog.

Nylabone Products
P.O. Box 427, Neptune NJ 07754-0427
Fax 732-988-5466
www.nylabone.com • info@nylabone.com
For more information contact your sales representative or contact us at sales@nylabone.com

CENTRAL
Garden & Pet